KU-652-298

THE CONGO - 1960
THE FIRST IRISH UNITED NATIONS PEACEKEEPERS

ARCHIE RAESIDE

Contents

Published in Ireland by
Arderin Publishing Company,
4 Parkview, Portlaoise, Co. Laois. (Tel: 0502 / 20356)

© Arderin Publishing Company
Published in 2004.

ISBN 0 86335 055 0 (paperback)
0 86335 056 9 (hardback)

All rights reserved. No part of this publication may be reproduced, stored in a retrieval system, or transmitted in any form or by any means electronic, photocopying, recording, or otherwise, without prior written permission of the publisher.

A catalogue record of this book is available from the British Library.

Front Cover: Actual helmet worn by the author in 1960.
Back Cover: Oil painting by native artist purchased by the author in Leopoldville (Kinshasa).

DESIGNED AND PRINTED BY LEINSTER LEADER LTD., NAAS, CO. KILDARE.
COVER DESIGN BY IAN DACK

A Word from the Author

For as long as I can remember I have been fascinated by aircraft and from about ten years of age I was building and flying scale models. As a teenager I knew that one day I would be a professional airman. I was accepted into the Technical Training Squadron of the Irish Air Corps in 1955 and, after qualifying as an airman, became a technical draughtsman in the Aeronautical Engineering section with Administrative Squadron.

One of my hobbies at that time, photography, led to an interest in movie film. Initially using a 9.5mm home-movie camera, I quickly progressed on to an 8mm Pailard Bolex with 300mm chrome finish zoom lens. Car racing in the Phoenix Park, the Mail Boat at Dunlaoghaire, the military parade through Dublin at Easter, aircraft at Dublin Airport and weddings were but a few of the subjects recorded. Spontaneous filming of my colleagues at Baldonnel as well as formal occasions such as the Commissioning and Wings presentation ceremony (followed by a showing) soon earned me a reputation as the Camp moviemaker.

With the availability of easy-to-use Camcorders in the last decade or two, it is perhaps difficult for the younger generation to appreciate the magic of film in its original form. It may be worth mentioning that the time I write about is pre-Irish Television (RTE). Cinephotographers were thin on the ground and the family camera was the Kodak Brownie.

In July 1960, the United Nations requested that Ireland send a peacekeeping force to help restore order in the Congo. When the call went out for volunteers the response was tremendous, with over three thousand officers, NCO's and men, each hoping to be one of the 689 required to form the first battalion in the history of the present day army to serve overseas. Due to heavy flying commitments and low personnel numbers, the Air Corps was excluded from volunteering. Although there were many disappointed people at Baldonnel, great credit must go to every one involved for their part in what was to be the biggest military airlift ever in Ireland. Every task was carried out in high spirits with professionalism and skill, as preparations got under way to receive the big American troop carriers commissioned to transport the troops.

After the initial disappointment of not being permitted to volunteer, my comrades and I in the Drawing Office settled down to our normal routine. Flight Sergeant Kevin Brown (KB) entered the office and from behind the security counter (the Drawing Office was a restricted area) he announced that the Officer Commanding, Air Corps, Colonel W.J. Keane, wished to see me. Checking that my tunic was properly buttoned-up, I hurried along the polished corridors desperately trying to figure out the reason for this call from on high. On reaching the door, I knocked, waited for the green light to show, and entered. Observing that the Colonel was holding the telephone handset, my thoughts raced as I continued to try and figure out what it was he wanted. Directly the Colonel addressed

I begin filming at the Curragh Military Camp.

me. "Airman Raeside, would you like to go to the Congo?" Surely I was dreaming, did I hear him correctly? After a brief hesitation I said, "As what, Sir?" He then told me that the army required a cine camera-man and as soon as I said "Yes, Sir" he spoke into the telephone and said, "I have your man, Jack".

The next morning I sat opposite Captain Jack Millar at Red House, General Headquarters at Parkgate. Being the last to be interviewed for the job, he was able to confirm my appointment. As I drove back out the Naas Road to Baldonnel, with the hood of my car down, I recall singing aloud. The new Battalion was already forming up and making preparations for the move out, so I was collected in the afternoon by a staff car from GHQ, taken to the Curragh Military Camp and my work began immediately. Issued with a clock-work-driven 16mm cine-camera, a tripod and some magazines of colour film, I moved around the Curragh Camp filming the activities of the Battalion in the closing days of the preparations for departure.

The equipment available to the Army in 1960 was of Second World War vintage and this applied, not just to the one camera with which I was issued, but to the sections involved as well, including transport and engineering.

In order to take still photographs I used my own 35mm Super Baldina and Yasica 44 and left instructions for my personal dark room equipment to be forwarded separately. This eventually arrived during the week of our return to Ireland, six months later.

A civilian press corps travelled with the troops and stayed for a short while in the Congo, sending dispatches to their newspapers on how the Irish were settling into their new environment. This was a great help to the anxious relatives and friends back home, hungry for news of their loved ones, four thousand miles away. Gay O'Brien of the Irish Independent donated his film processing and printing and enlarging equipment to the Battalion when he left the Congo after a couple of weeks. On a voluntary basis I was then in a position to process photographs for the members of both Battalions.

In response to the ongoing and surprisingly continuous interest by people of all ages in the events of the Irish in the Congo four decades ago, this book, drawn from my own records, illustrates those activities in the areas of the Congo where I served. It is fortunate that I kept a daily log-book, or diary, a habit developed as a Scout Leader and what I have written in these pages are based on my diary. My story is, therefore, that of one individual soldier engaged on an extraordinary, mould-breaking adventure that paved the way for numerous other peace-keeping missions in the future. The benefit of forty years of United Nations service has brought about many advances in training, equipment and an overall approach to peacekeeping and the Irish men and women, who have contributed to peace in many parts of the world, have done Ireland proud.

I dedicate this book to all who served in the Congo and especially to those who gave their lives in the service of peace.

Archie Raeside

Acknowledgements

I thank my wife Mary Bernadette, known to all as Bernie, for the happy 42 years that we have shared, for her wisdom and for her tolerance and patience of my varied activities and interests.

To my children and their spouses and my grandchildren I thank them for their support and encouragement in this and other projects.

I thank Teddy Fennelly, my friendly editor, for his faith in my book and for his patience, skill and professionalism in making it a reality.

To Carmel and the Fennelly family for the warm welcome extended to me.

To Ian Dack, my daughter Bernadette's husband, for his artistic skills in producing the cover design.

To Joan Phelan, my local librarian, for her interest and the friendship she and Mick have extended to Bernie and myself.

To Liam Murphy, P.R.O. Post no. 11, United Nations Veterans' Association, for his support and Joe Mallon, John Hanlon and William Duffy for relating their memories.

I would also like to thank Comdts Pat Brennan and Victor Laing of Military Archives, Paddy McLoughlin, Casement Branch O.N.E.T., Lt. Col. Jim Goulding, U.N. Training School Curragh, and all my former comrades for their help and encouragement.

Thanks to the various newspapers for allowing me to reproduce some cuttings relating to the period.

Roll of Honour

This is the Roll of Honour of the twenty-seven Irish soldiers who lost their lives during the Irish peacekeeping mission in the Congo 1960-'64 and to whom this book is dedicated:

C/S Felix Grant
Col. Justin McCarthy
Lt. Kevin Gleeson
Sgt. Hugh Gaynor
Cpl. Peter Kelly
Cpl. Liam Dougan
Pte. Matt Farrell
Tpr. Tom Fennell
Tpr. Anthony Browne
Pte. Michael McGuinn
Pte. Gerry Killeen
Pte. Patrick Davis
Cpl. Liam Kelly
Cpl. Luke Kelly

Tpr. Edward Gaffney
Tpr. Patrick Mullins
Cpl. Michael Nolan
FSO Frank Eivers
Cpl. Michael Fallon
Sgt. Patrick Mulcahy
Pte. Andrew Wickham
Lt. Paddy Riordan
Cpl. John Geoghegan
Cpl. John Power
Capt. Dick McCann
Cpl. Jack McCarthy
Comdt. Malachy McMahon

Tributes

The Congo experience was of "inestimable value" to the Army
"The experience gained by all ranks is of inestimable value while at home, at all levels of command and administration, the Congo Operation has provided a wealth of experience. The organization, training, equipping, supply, maintenance and administration (both personnel and logistical) of contingents of service with the UN has been absorbed into the normal routine of military command and military staff functions and many useful lessons have been learned. The overall general effect has been to create a more efficient and flexible military structure."
An Cosantoir, July 1964

US President Bill Clinton on Ireland's contribution to the UN
"I would like to say, because I can't leave Ireland without acknowledging this, that there are few nations that have contributed more than Ireland, even in times which were difficult for this country, to the cause of peace and human rights around the world. ... Since peacekeeping began for the United Nations 40 years ago, 75 Irish soldiers have given their lives. Today we work shoulder to shoulder in Bosnia and the Middle East but I think you should know that as nearly as I can determine, in the 40 years in which the world has been working together on peacekeeping, the only country in the world which has never taken a single, solitary day off from the cause of world peace in the United Nations peacekeeping operations is Ireland. And I thank you."

Tribute by Seán Lemass (Taoiseach 1959-'66)
" ... Gallant Irish soldiers have died in Niemba, Elizabethville and elsewhere in that troubled land as many of their comrades in other contingents comprising the United Nations force have also died. We ask the Almighty God to reward their sacrifice by guiding the leaders of all nations on the road to peace based on justice, and to inspire the leaders of the Congo peoples to a reasonable solution of their difficulties in a way which will make further help from other nations no longer necessary.

"If our prayer is answered, people in many lands, speaking in many tongues, will give thanks to God that men like these, whom we now honour, were ready to take risks which the cause they served necessarily involved. So long as the Irish nation serves these high principles, so long will their names be remembered, and in the ranks of our Irish Army their memory will always be kept in honour."

The Democratic Republic of the Congo

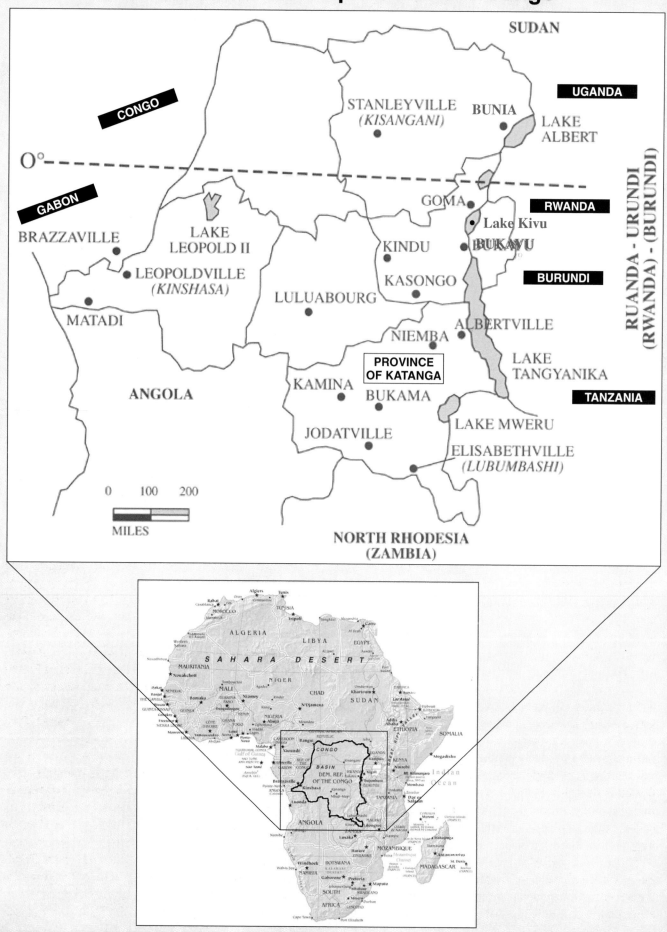

Introduction

By Teddy Fennelly

The Irish Army's peacekeeping involvement in the Congo (ONUC) began with the dispatch of the 32nd Battalion in July 1960 and ended with the repatriation of the 2nd Infantry Group in May 1964. Each unit served a six-month tour of duty.

The newly liberated Congo had become a pawn in the politics of the Cold War The mineral-rich breakaway province of Katanga was a smoking gun that threatened to plunge the whole country into a bloody civil war. It was the task of the Irish, and the peacemakers from other countries, to prevent bloodshed and to keep the country united. The tangled web of internal and external political intrigues at play in the Congo further complicated an already difficult and risky mission.

Apart from a short briefing prior to their departure, the vast majority of the Irish soldiers knew little or nothing about the Congo, or about the volatile and dangerous environment into which they were being plunged.

Neither was their task helped by the UN mandate, which was unclear especially relating to the use of force. The UN forces were sent in to keep the peace in a country in which everybody seemed to be spoiling for fight. To keep the protagonists from each other's throats, the peacekeepers had sometimes to intervene in local conflicts yet they had to ensure that their actions did not favour one side or the other in any given situation. Their every action was open to criticism by rival combatants inside the Congo and by the influential vested interests on the international stage. They lacked an adequate intelligence back-up, which this highly sensitive situation demanded, and they carried out their tasks in a high risk situation, with the enemy monitoring their every move and dangers lurking everywhere.

The Irish soldiers, dressed on their departure in their bull's-wool uniforms which were totally unsuited to the tropical climate, and ill-equipped with home-made armoured cars and obsolete weapons, performed remarkably well in the circumstances. Their personnel showed resourcefulness and raw courage when needed and helped defuse countless flashpoint situations between rival factions in various volatile areas of the Congo.

The Irish carried out their important peacekeeping mission commendably but at a high cost. Twenty-seven of her soldiers lost their lives there. They died in the service of their country and of mankind. It is quite amazing that this figure, regrettable as it is, was not far greater in view of their exposure to danger in such a hostile and alien environment. That, in itself, is a tribute to the calibre, discipline and professionalism of the officers and men involved.

It is quite remarkable that all 689 soldiers of the 32nd Battalion, the first detachment of Irish troops sent to the Congo in July 1960, of which the author was a member, returned safely to their country six months later. The next contingent, the 33rd Battalion, which served their term for the most part alongside the 32nd, was not as fortunate. The ambush on one of its units by Baluba tribesmen at Niemba in November of that year, left nine Irish soldiers dead and shocked the Irish nation.

The Baluba were not the main threat to the Irish in Katanga, however. The secessionist gerdarmerie led by white mercenaries resented UN intervention into the breakaway province. A year after Niemba, men from the 36th Battalion backed by units from the 35th, were sent in to seize and hold a railway tunnel from Katangan rebels. The tunnel was a vital artery for access to Elizabethville, the Katangan capital. It provided good cover for the rebels who rained mortar and machine gunfire on their attackers.° The tunnel was cleared of rebels after a fierce battle, which claimed the lives of three soldiers, Lieut. Paddy Riordan, platoon commander, Artillery Sgt. Paddy Mulcahy, DSM, from Tipperary, and radio operator, Pte. Andrew Wickham, from Wexford.

This was a major success for the Irish Army in the

field of combat. Its soldiers had won for themselves and their country international acclaim. As time passed Irish units were engaged in other fields of combat during the Congo operation and unfortunately there were to be further casualties sustained.

The brave young men who died in the Congo and in other foreign fields will, deservedly, forever hold a place of honour in Irish history. But, for some yet unknown reason, the feats of other brave Irish soldiers, who survived the Congo experience against overwhelming odds, have been airbrushed from our history.

These were the heroes of the Battle of Jadotville, which took place in September 1961, a mere two months prior to the tunnel engagement. A company of 150 Irish peacekeepers of the Western Command, attached to the 35th Battalion, were deployed on a dubious mission to protect foreigners, mostly Belgian, in the dusty mining town of Jadotville in the heart of the troubled breakaway province of Katanga. The foreigners were there of their own volition. They did not seek UN help nor did they welcome it. Instead of a welcome for the Irish soldiers at Jadotville they got a hostile reception from the Katanganese and foreigners alike.

Anger soon turned to aggression. The unit was attacked by a well-armed and superior force of an estimated 2,000 rebel troops under the command of white mercenaries. The battle waged for five days until the Irish contingent ran out of food, water and ammunition. Forced to surrender or risk immediate annihilation of his company, the officer commanding, Comdt. Pat Quinlan, negotiated safe passage for his troops and, after a short time in captivity, they were released under a prisoner exchange arrangement. Although hundreds of the local troops were killed in the fierce fighting, quite remarkably the Irish suffered no fatalities.

But for the effectiveness and courage of the men in combat and the astuteness of their commanding officer, the episode could have resulted in the disastrous loss of many lives. The gallantry and military skills displayed by the Irish during the Battle of Jadotville must rank as one of the Irish Army's proudest achievements, yet the bravery and professionalism of the officers and men have never been recognised by the country or its people.

Questions have been asked as to why this small lightly armed company was left so exposed for so long and why an adequate and timely rescue operation was not mounted. At the time of going to print, a board of military officers are examining a submission from a retired army officer who served in the Congo in 1961. Hopefully this will result in the heroes of Jadotville, and their remarkable story of survival, being fully acknowledged and duly recorded with pride in our history books.

The authority of the central government was gradually established and by mid-1963 the UN operation was being wound up. The last of the Irish soldiers were repatriated in May 1964.

Despite the shortcomings it experienced, the Irish Army proved itself a competent military force and its role in the Congo was acclaimed by the UN and world leaders. It, perhaps more so than any of the other foreign units, was seen and respected as peacekeepers, who did the job it was deployed to do. It also played a significant role in ensuring that the Congo's wealthiest province, Katanga, was not allowed to sunder itself from the mother nation.

Less acknowledged, however, is the impact that the success of the mission had on the Irish nation. Ireland in the 1950s was a poverty-ridden depressing country, disemboweled of its youth through emigration. There was little in its society or in its institutions that nurtured confidence or pride in its own relatively new nationhood. Then along came the 1960s and an era of rapid modernisation under Sean Lemass, who became Taoiseach in 1959. Ireland slowly emerged from the economic and social stagnation of the post-Independence decades and opened its doors to the world.

The Congo experience complemented the emergence of a confident and prosperous new Ireland. "Operation Sarsfield" gave Ireland the exposure it needed on the world stage. Here was perceived a small island country on the outer edge of Europe with a highly effective military force, fighting in a foreign land not to win a war but rather to establish peace. The Irish Army restored the self-esteem to a demoralized nation and, for that, this country and its people should be forever grateful.

Each soldier who served on "Operation Sarsfield", could tell his own story and recount his own personal experiences. Surprisingly few have done so. The author, Archie Raeside, is an exception. That is why this book is so important.

Prologue

Casement and the Congo

Henry Morton Stanley, explored the Congo River Basin between 1874 and 1880. His reports stimulated great interest in the area, particularly as a source of rubber and mineral wealth. King Leopold II of Belgium engaged Stanley to establish trading stations and friendly relations with the native people. The King set up the Congo Free State in 1885 and he became its personal sovereign. "I don't want to miss the chance of getting us a slice of this magnificent African cake", he said in a letter to one of his ambassadors. He viewed the raw materials and the people of the Congo as a prize to be consumed. But even by the standards of the day, Leopold's behaviour was abominable. The appalling treatment of rubber tappers – there were massacres, possibly of millions, and mutilation of "offenders" who failed to deliver enough rubber – was exposed in a report by the British Consul, Roger Casement. This resulted in international outrage which led the Belgian Parliament to take control of the Congo in 1908, and it became a colony known as the Belgian Congo. Roger Casement was knighted in 1911 for his services to humanity both in the Congo and later in Brazil, where he exposed similar exploitation of the native people. In 1916 he was executed in London as a traitor for trying to enlist German support for the Irish nationalist movement.

The Congo – "a country of cannibals, slaves and savagery"

The perception of the Congo a half-century ago was drawn largely from newspaper articles, jungle books and Tarzan films. The very name of the Congo conjured up images of vast rain forest, endless bush, giant rivers, rumbling volcanoes and mystic mountains, stretching more than a thousand miles from its Atlantic coastline into the dark heart of Africa. This was the land of the elephant, rhino and lion king, of slithery poisonous snakes lurking in the undergrowth, of exotic birds up every tree and of clouds of ravaging locusts that turned the day into night. The strange smells and sounds were synonymous with this weird and wonderful landscape.

But what about its people? The Congo was perceived as an immense country full of smaller kingdoms, where primitive and warlike tribes, ranging from giants to pygmies, armed with spears and poison arrows, defended their patch against marauding neighbours on a daily basis. The warriors paid tribute to their chief and obeyed his every command but were under the spell and influence of the local witch-doctor, who prescribed a magical potion for every ailment and used curious incense-like concoctions to embellish his devilish prognostications.

Perhaps the defining image of the Congolese to the Irish man and woman in the street in July 1960 was the one encapsulated in a newspaper headline of the period. It described it as a country of "cannibals, slaves and savagery".

Katanga wants out

The flame of freedom and self-determination swept through the African continent in the 1950s and '60s as the age of colonialism drew to a close. The new states were ill prepared for independence and, as the colonizers salvaged whatever they could for themselves when withdrawing from the turmoil, the native populations were left starved of the resources and personnel to effectively run their countries. Inevitably many found their countries plunged into bloody civil war, the sad legacy of colonialism. To make matters worse, the Cold War was at its height and with the two superpowers, the US and USSR, trying to outflank each other, the emerging states were used as pawns in a global conflict not of their making. This further exacerbated the mistrust and divisions that already existed between different tribes and ethnic groups.

Token reforms towards Congolese self-government had been initiated in the late 1950s but few of the Congolese were educated and the Belgians did little to pave the way for independence. Typical of other African colonies, the Congo was comprised of diverse tribal groupings, lacking all but the most rudimentary mechanisms or understanding of government.

The flames of freedom in the Congo were fanned by a period of nationalist riots, which unnerved the Belgians. Independence was declared on 30 June 1960 and the country changed its name to the Republic of the Congo. It was governed initially by its President, Joseph Kasavubu, and Prime Minister, Patrice Lumumba. Shortly after gaining independence a military mutiny against the white, and mostly Belgian, officer corps took place. A hitherto little-known Congolese Army officer, Joseph Mobutu, was appointed as army chief-of-staff. As the military insurrection spread, the Belgian civil servants began to flee the country, which prompted intervention by Belgian troops.

In July 1960, Congolese rebel leader, Moise Tshombe, supported by the Belgians, declared the mining rich province of Katanga as an independent state under his leadership. Kasavubu and Lumumba appealed to the Secretary-General of the UN, Dag Hammarskjold, for military assistance to restore order and to prevent a break-up in the newly independent country.

Ireland's Call

The first UN intervention unit to hit the scene was from Ghana, still bathing in its reputation as the first African nation to win its freedom. The force was strengthened by support initially from predominately African countries with Tunisia, Morocco, Ethiopia, Guinea and Liberia sending in their troops. The first white units came from neutral countries, Sweden and Ireland.

Ireland had joined the UN only five years previously and the powers-that-be were determined to project a progressive image for the country on the world stage. The Congo provided a suitable platform. The Irish Government and Army were delighted to be asked to play an international peacekeeping role with the UN and by early August 1960 there were 1,400 Irish soldiers on active service in the Congo. The mission, codenamed 'Operation Sarsfield', captured the imagination of the Irish public and the story dominated the headlines for the months and even years ahead. The Irish had distinguished themselves as fearless fighters in foreign armies on every continent but this was the first time for Irish soldiers in Irish Army uniform to face active combat on a foreign field. It was a challenge that was taken up enthusiastically by the Irish troops. Eventually twenty-eight countries contributed a total of 20,000 to the peacekeeping mission, which lasted four years.

Mobutu comes to power

As divisions continued to grow in the Congolese government and between the multitude of ethnic groups, Mobutu exploited the splits and the lack of trust that prevailed to gradually enhance his own position. He had Lumumba arrested and handed him over to the Katangans who had him murdered in February 1961.

The Irish diplomat, Conor Cruise O'Brien, was appointed by Hammarskjold as the chief UN representative in Katanga that same year. Cruise O'Brien opposed the secession of the Congo's wealthiest province from the rest of the country and by doing so run foul of the US, Belgium, France and Britain interests. The plot thickened when Dag Hammarskjold was killed in suspicious circumstances in an air crash near Ndola, Zambia, in September 1961, while engaged in negotiations over the Congo crisis. Sabotage has still not been ruled out. He was replaced as UN Secretary General by U Thant of Burma.

Cruise O'Brien was forced to resign from his UN post after a dirty-tricks campaign against him by vested interests in the West and in Africa. In 1962 he published his best-known book, *To Katanga and Back*, which exposed the intrigues at play in the Congo.

By 1964 the main objective of the UN mission had been achieved: the integrity of the new state had been preserved. But the struggle for power continued. The Congolese National Army, under the leadership of Mobutu, suppressed a rising headed by Tshombe, who had declared himself Prime Minister, in 1964. Mobutu seized power in November 1965 and was elected President five years later. In 1971 the country was renamed Zaire and Mobutu's party, the Popular Movement of the Revolution, was declared the only legal political party.

Mobutu was a ruthless and corrupt despot, similar to King Leopold almost a century earlier, until his overthrow in 1997. As he stashed much of the country's economic output in European banks, Zaire became the most notorious example of a country where state institutions came to be little more than a way of delivering money to the ruling elite. The politics of the Cold War ensured him Western backing. It took the end of the Cold War – followed by the Rwandan genocide – to prompt a successful revolution against his regime.

Kabila's coup and its aftermath

The coup was led by Laurent Kabila, who declared himself President and changed the name of the country to the Democratic Republic of the Congo. The country's problems were far from over, however. A Goma based rebel group, the Congolese Rally for Democracy, attempted to take control of the country's capital, Kinshasa, but were repulsed. The rebels did succeed, however, in taking control of virtually the entire east side of the country, causing 700,000 refugees to flee the war zone. Between 1998 and 2000, nine countries were sucked into a war that fractured the Congo and divided the continent of Africa. An estimated 3 to 5 million people have been slaughtered in the holocaust, the bloodiest conflict since WWII. But with the ending of the Cold War, the Congo was no longer of any strategic importance to the one remaining superpower or to the West and its grim plight was ignored and the dreadful bloodshed went largely unreported.

In January 2001, President Kabila, was killed in a coup and he was replaced by his son, Joseph (31), as Head of State. The young Kabila has co-operated with UN Security attempts to negotiate a peace settlement between the rival factions in the Congo and between the other African countries caught up in the conflict. A new UN peacekeeping operation was initiated and, in May 2003, Irish troops were reported to be on stand-by awaiting a call-up to join the mission. Ireland's call on this occasion, however, was destined for another troubled African country, Liberia, and in November 2003 a total of 430 Irish soldiers forming a motorized infantry battalion as well as military observers and a special Rangers unit embarked on another dangerous mission.

Forty years after the last Irish troops of "Operation Sarsfield" concluded their mission in the Congo, it is a case of *déjà vu*. Despite the presence of 10,000 peacekeeping troops there, chaos remains the order of the day. This time the UN intervention is a case of too little too late. The slaughter continues as the world stands idly by.

Irish Units in the Congo (1960-'64)

32nd Infantry Battalion – Lt. Col. Buckley
33rd Infantry Battalion – Lt. Col. Bunworth
34th Infantry Battalion – Lt. Col. O'Neill
1st Infantry Group – Lt. Col. O'Donovan
35th Infantry Battalion – Lt. Col. McNeill/
   Lt. Col. McNamee
36th Infantry Battalion – Lt. Col. Hogan/
   Lt. Col. Ryan
37th Infantry Battalion – Lt. Col. O'Broin
2nd Armoured Car Squadron – Comdt. Foley
38th Infantry Battalion – Lt. Col. Delaney

3rd Armoured Car Squadron – Comdt. Cahalane
39th Infantry Battalion – Lt. Col. Dempsey
2nd Infantry Group – Lt. Col. O'Sullivan

A total of 5,237 Irish military personnel served in the Congo, including 754 personnel who served twice and 154 who served three times.

The Irish Army Chief-of-Staff, Lt. General Sean McKeown, held the appointment of Force Commander ONUC from January 1961 to March 1962.

Chapter 1

"I'm off to the Congo"

For the families and friends of the soldiers of the 32nd Battalion, those words came as a complete shock. Never before had an Irish army embarked on an overseas mission, and the Congo assignment in central Africa was, probably, as tough and as dangerous as they come. We soldiers, on the other hand, were very excited by the prospect of service on foreign soil and it was a big disappointment for those who volunteered but were not selected to take part in 'Operation Sarsfield' – the military name given to the mission. The feeling throughout the country was one of pride at the prospect of Ireland's participation in helping to bring peace to a war-torn and much exploited poverty stricken country.

Little time for farewells
For most of the members of the Battalion there was little time for farewell parties. Within hours of being selected, in some cases, soldiers were on their way to the Curragh Military Camp, where men from practically every county in Ireland came together to form the 32nd United Nations Infantry Battalion. There was a great sense of camaraderie and unity in evidence. With such little time to get organised before departure, there was also a strong feeling of urgency. Injections against smallpox, yellow fever and malaria were administered, and the dentist was kept very busy. Everybody was x-rayed and short wills were signed. After all it wasn't a holiday the boys were going on.

The 32nd Battalion mobilising for the Congo mission.

First briefing

On the 25 July 1960, just two days before takeoff, the 689-strong Battalion was assembled in the Curragh and given a first briefing by our commanding officer, Lieutenant Colonel Mortimer Buckley. In his address, he said: "We are going on a mission for friends. Remember, when you get to the Congo, that everyone is your friend until they prove otherwise, and when it's all over I hope that we all come home safely again". He said he felt honoured to lead the men and he hoped that they were fully aware of the honour that had been bestowed on them by being selected to serve with the unit. His address also included cautionary advice on food, water, and proper complaint procedures, as well as the need to take great care of weapons. As we left the hall for breakfast, we gave our new commanding officer a rousing cheer.

Flag presented

A silken green flag with a purple centre was presented to the Battalion on behalf of the women of the Curragh, by Mrs. Maura Donagh. The flag also featured crossed golden rifles, which were encircled by the words Cathalan Eireann (Irish Battalion) and the number 32. This was the first of many such flags to be borne by Irish peacekeeping troops for the next forty years and more.

Up to the end of WW2 (or the Emergency, as the period was known in Ireland) there had been thirty-one battalions within the Irish Defence Forces. This was a new battalion drawn from various units, brigades, commands, corps, and services, and thus became known as the 32nd – hence the number on the flag.

Meeting with Dev

On the eve of our departure I travelled with officers of the Battalion in a military bus to Aras an Uachtarain in the Phoenix Park. I filmed the historic event as President Eamon de Valera and senior Government Ministers received the Officer Corps and wished them well in leading this historic first overseas operation for the Irish Army.

The 32nd Battalion build-up continues.

The Advance Party

An advance party of the 32nd Battalion had flown to the Congo on the 23rd July, to prepare the way for the main body of men who would be arriving a few days later. These included four officers, six non-commissioned officers (NCOs), seven interpreters and an United Nations Political Adviser. They were led by Commandant Joseph J. Adams, second in command of the Battallion, and Commandant Joseph Laffan, senior medical officer.

On arrival in Leopoldville on the following day, they were taken by speedboat across the river to the office of General Van Horn, the Swedish Military Commander of the UN force in the Congo. The General, who had overall command of all the forces, including the Irish, welcomed them and they discussed the requirements of the 32nd Battallion.

Change of plan

Initially the Irish troops were to be deployed in the Coquilhatville (now Mbandaka) region, a low-lying swamp area in the northwest of the country, which was infested with mosquitoes and hookworm. The Chief Medical Officer of the UN advised against placing white troops here, however, especially when there was no mosquito netting or long-range radio equipment available. Instead the area of operations for the Irish contingent was relocated to the Kivu province, on the east side of this vast country, on the borders of Rwanda and Burundi.

The change in location created some extra problems, such as the greater distance from Leopoldville to Goma in the Kivu province, over a thousand miles, and the need for high powered radio equipment, which up to then had been unavailable. As was the case in Coquilhatville, there was little or no information on the situation, with regards conflict, in the Kivu province.

The advance party used Monday, 25 July, to gather intelligence about the Kivu region prior to travelling there. Missionaries, truck drivers, Sabena pilots and commercial firms in Goma, Bukavu and Kindu, were consulted in order to form a precise picture of the situation in the region. Information was obtained on the strength of the Belgian and Congolese forces, the availability of supplies and transport, and the condition of the roads infrastructure there.

Goma Airport

While final preparations were underway back in Ireland for the airlift of the entire 32nd Battalion, the advance party was faced with the increasingly urgent task of securing the airport in Goma, and testing the reaction of the local people and the military to the operation.

In the early hours of Thursday, 28 July, three Sabena aircraft were made available to the Irish advance party. With the help of some Swedish troops, two of the aircraft were loaded with stores while the third contained the advance party as well as some stores, which were to be offloaded in Kindu before continuing on to Goma. The landing at Kindu was uneventful and Captain Liddy, one NCO, and two Swedish interpreters remained there to meet a company of the main body, which was due soon from Ireland.

The remainder of the party, which by now also included two pressmen, Cathal O Shannon from the Irish Times, and Michael O'Halloran, from the Irish Press, flew on towards Goma. Just minutes from their destination, the pilot received a radio message from one of the two aircraft that had flown direct, and had landed some time earlier. It reported that Congolese troops at the airport were hostile and had commandeered all the cargo from both aircraft. They were also aware of the approaching third aircraft and intended holding the advance party as prisoners.

Local hostility

This message was conveyed to Commandant Adams and the pilot requested a diversion to Usumbura in Ruanda Urundi (now Rwanda and Burundi). Commandant Adams refused, however, and instructed the pilot to land at Goma as per the agreed charter instructions.

The aircraft landed in Goma and rolled to a halt without incident. When the door opened, the occupants were met by the amazing sight of over 300 armed Congolese troops, 50 armed police and about 10,000 people. From the elevated position of the aircraft steps, Commandant Adams explained the aims and the intentions of the United Nations, to the suspicious natives. It was agreed to discuss the matter further in the airport building.

In attendance at this conference were the Commandant of the Congolese Army, the Chief of Police, the Territorial Commissioner and the Local Administrator. Commandant Laffan reiterated the objectives of the United Nations and stated his requirements regarding transport and accommodation for the Irish peacekeeping troops. The return of the stores was also requested. After the conference, he made another speech from the steps of the airport building, briefly outlining the history of the Irish people and their attitude to colonialism. This seemed to pacify the civilian assembly but the military were still distrustful.

A military bus was made available and the advance party was taken to Goma town and to schools in the area, which might be used as a base for the Battalion. The local military camp was also visited and they were offered accommodation there. But because it had become abundantly clear that some of the Congolese officers and NCO's were in favour of keeping the advance party as prisoners, the offer was politely declined.

Reduced tensions

Instead Headquarters was established in the local hostelry, Grand Lacs Hotel. The senior Congolese people who had attended the earlier conference were invited to dinner there and this helped to reduce tensions. This was a good public relations exercise, as Congolese would not have been allowed into the hotel prior to independence. At the meal, the Congolese Commandant sat at the table with a submachine gun on his knees and hand grenades attached to his belt and for a while he wore his helmet and greatcoat. The cargoes, which had been commandeered on arrival, were returned to the Irish forces on the following morning.

By this stage, the first aircraft carrying part of the history-making 32nd Battalion of the Irish Army, with Commanding Officer, Lieutenant Colonel Mortimer Buckley, some senior officers and the army pipe band on board, was winging its way to Goma.

Time out

During the very busy week leading up to this historic day, I was given twenty-four hours leave of absence to bid farewell to my own family. The last port of call was to my girlfriend, Bernie's, home in Dalkey. We drove up to Killiney Head, something we had done many times before and sat with the hood of my MG sports car down, gazing at the stars in the sky and enjoying the lights of the city, spread out before us. We talked of our love for each other and speculated on how things might be in six months time when I returned. Looking back now, that six months period remains the longest time we have spent apart since we came to know each other.

Farewell date with my girlfriend Bernie Kennedy, now my wife of 42 years.

Swedish General To Head Five-Nation Force
U.N. "ARMY" FOR CONGO

U.S. Gives Stern Warning To Reds

Victorious Kennedy Proposes Johnson For 'Ticket'

A S jubilant Democrats acclaimed Senator John Fitzgerald Kennedy after his spectacular nomination as candidate for the Presidency of the United States, the young Senator caused a major surprise by announcing that Senator Lyndon Johnson had agreed to seek nomination as his vice-Presidential "running mate."

Senator Kennedy's surprise announcement as the Democratic candidate in Los Angeles last night surprised that Senator Johnson would be named as the vice-presidential candidate to start early this evening.

The Convention battle lasted nearly nine hours with the traditional wild and noisy scenes of carnival revelry, blaring bands and waving banners.

From the beginning, the chairman, Governor L. Collins of Florida, had to pound his gavel repeatedly to restore order.

KENNEDY ASKED.

At a Press conference Senator Kennedy said he had asked Senator Johnson to seek to stand as Vice-President, and that he agreed to do so.

Nomination of Senator Johnson as Senator Kennedy's running-mate would balance the Democratic "ticket." As a Southerner he would attract votes from the Southern wing of the Party. Equally, Senator Johnson is a Protestant, and this, to some extent, balances the fact that Senator Kennedy is a Catholic.

Even Senator Kennedy, the

43-year-old Catholic from Boston, romped home on the first ballot with 806 votes compared with 409 for his nearest rival. Senator Lyndon Johnson of Texas. Other delegates tried to switch their votes to Kennedy but were too late for the official count.

UNITY SPEECH

After the vote, the defeated candidates promised to unite behind the winner. Senator Johnson's speech urging the party to unite behind Senator Kennedy said: "Let us sweep the country so that in January democratic leadership may be restored to America."

Senator Kennedy's success was acclaimed with wild enthusiasm by 20,000 spectators and delegates. He told the Convention: "I hope I will be worthy of your trust. We shall win."

Nomination of the boyish-looking Senator left his wife, Jacqueline, breathing as she heard the news at their summer home in Hyannis, Massachusetts. "I am very excited about it, of course," she said. But on doctor's orders she is expecting a child in November—she would not fly out to the Convention "much as I would like to."

Her husband will almost certainly fight out the contest for the Presidency with Republican Vice-President Nixon, and officials on both sides say they expect one of the toughest and hardest fought Presidential elections campaigns of the century.

Senator John F. Kennedy chosen to be the Democratic candidate for the Presidency of the United States.

Shipping Strike
GOVERNMENT NOT TO INTERVENE

WHEN Mr. Cosgrave (F.G.) asked the Minister for Industry and Commerce at Question Time in the Dail if he would make a statement about the present dispute which was affecting passenger, tourist and freight shipping services at the Dublin port, Mr. Lynch stated that he did not propose to intervene

Mr. Lynch said that the dispute involving clerical workers employed by the British and Irish Steam Packet Co. had been the subject of a recommendation by the Labour Court.

Since the passing of the Industrial Relations Act 1946, it had not been the practice for members of the Government to intervene in trade disputes, and he did not propose to depart from that practice in the present instance.

journed until Monday. It seemed to be somewhat casual that the matter should be adjourned until Monday, in view of the serious consequences of a continuation of the strike.

Mr. Lynch said that the latest information he had was that the parties were endeavouring to come together that afternoon.

Mr. Cosgrave said that it had been announced earlier that the discussions had been adjourned until Monday.

Katanga Rejects New Move

THE first contingent of United Nations forces for the Congo — made up of African troops under a Swedish general — will arrive in Leopoldville within 48 hours, the U.N. Secretary-General has announced.

At the same time Belgium sought the U.N.'s help to avoid a clear break with the Congo. The Belgian delegate to the U.N. Mr. Loridan, said the Congo had cabled Belgium it had broken off relations.

The rupture would mean, said Mr. Loridan that, what protection Belgium's diplomatic missions had given to Belgians in the Congo would come to an end.

WILL REPLACE BELGIANS

In Leopoldville Dr. Ralphe Bunche, Deputy Under-Secretary of the United Nations, told a Press Conference that the U.N. troops would be armed only with "defensive weapons" and under the provisions of the Security Council Resolution would replace the Belgian troops now in the Congo.

The first contingent would be

made up of troops from Ghana, Guinea, the Mali Federation (Sudan and Senegal) and Tunisia and would be under the command of General Karl Van Horn, of Sweden.

A Belgian Embassy spokesman in Leopoldville said the Belgian troops already in the country would be withdrawn progressively as the U.N. troops arrived.

KATANGA REFUSES AID

News of the U.N. intervention was not welcomed in Katanga province which has seceded from the Congo.

Mr. Moïse Tshombe, President of the Katanga Government, said he has cabled the U.N. Secretary General that he will not allow U.N. troops to enter the Katanga province. He said Belgian troops are efficiently maintaining order.

"A Diabolical Plan"

IN BRUSSELS, Mr. M. Eyskens, the Prime Minister, told the Belgian Parliament that the "sensational collapse of the Force Publique" had been prepared and directed from outside.

"An invisible hand tries to implement a treacherous and diabolical plan in attempting to provoke a generalised revolt in the Congo through lack of food," he said.

When M. Eyskens read extracts from the Soviet statement accusing the Belgian Government of

imperialism and aggression and expressed his Government's indignation at these accusations, he was applauded by both Government and Socialist opposition benches.

The only two Communist deputies were booed when one of them made an indistinct remark.

The Prime Minister then said: "The Government proclaims its indignation in front of a unanimous chamber except for the servants of a regime whose cynical bestiality is well known."

POPE TO GIVE AUDIENCES TWICE A WEEK

TO accommodate the thousands of tourists visiting Rome, the Holy Father will give twice-weekly general audiences during the summer months.

The Vatican Press Office said that such audiences will be given on Wednesday and Saturday in Rome and at Castel Gandolfo where the Pope will soon go to his summer residence. The twice-weekly audiences will begin on July 27. Normally, one weekly general audience is given each Wednesday.

The Vatican Press Office also announced that, during the same period, the Pontiff will recite the Angelus each Sunday at noon and at noon on August 15, feast of the Assumption. An amplifier hook-up will carry his voice both to tourists and pilgrims in St. Peter's Square and at Castel Gandolfo.

200 DIE AS FIRE SWEEPS ASYLUM

AT least 200 mental patients, many of them locked in their cells, died in a fire in the National Insane Asylum in Guatemala.

It is feared that the final death toll may be even higher. Five hundred others were trapped for a time but were rescued by firemen.

The fire broke out shortly after midnight and quickly swept through the old building which housed 1,100 inmates.

About 300 were trapped in the inner part of the building. Firemen, police and volunteers were unable to get all of the inmates out. Police said many of those burned to death were locked in cells.

INMATES ESCAPE

About 300 inmates, including several classified as criminally

THE United States re-affirming the Monroe doctrine warned the Soviet Union yesterday to keep its hands off Western Hemisphere countries.

At the same time, the U.S. State Department denounced as a "naked menace to world peace" Mr. Khrushchev's implied threats that Soviet rockets might fly to help Cuba repel alleged American aggression.

In a strongly-worded statement, the State Department accused Mr. Khrushchev of seeking to supplant the 137-year-old Monroe Doctrine providing for the use of Soviet military power in support of Communist movements anywhere in the world.

"HYPOCRISY REVEALED"

Mr. Khrushchev's threats, the Department said, revealed the hypocrisy of his protestations on behalf of peace.

President Eisenhower personally approved the Department declaration which was read to reporters by a Department spokesman at a Press conference in Washington.

With its warning against meddling in Western Hemisphere matters, the State Department replied to Mr. Khrushchev at a Press conference comments in Moscow on Tuesday when he said the Monroe Doctrine was dead and should be buried.

"STRAW MAN"

Speaking of Mr. Khrushchev's statements of July 9 and July 12 the statement said: "As a pretext for his threat, he conjured up the straw man of a non-existent menace of U.S. aggression against Cuba.

The threat of the use of force made so blatantly by the Soviet Chairman in relation to the affairs of nations of the Western Hemisphere is contrary to the basic principles of the United Nations charter which rejects the use of force in the settlement of international disputes.

As Mr. White was reading the statement it was announced in Washington that the Council of the Organisation of American States would meet to-morrow to consider Peru's request for a Foreign Ministers' conference to discuss tensions between the U.S. and Cuba.

President James Monroe gave a message to the U.S. Congress on December 2, 1823, to warn European nations against seeking to extend their system to the Western hemisphere.

CASTRO OFFICER ESCAPES BULLETS

Meanwhile, in Cuba, gunmen attempted to assassinate Major Nogueira Ramet, President of Dr. Castro's Military Tribunal, in Pinar del Rio Province.

Police said seven men armed with pistols fired on Major

[Irish Independent, Friday, 15 July 1960]

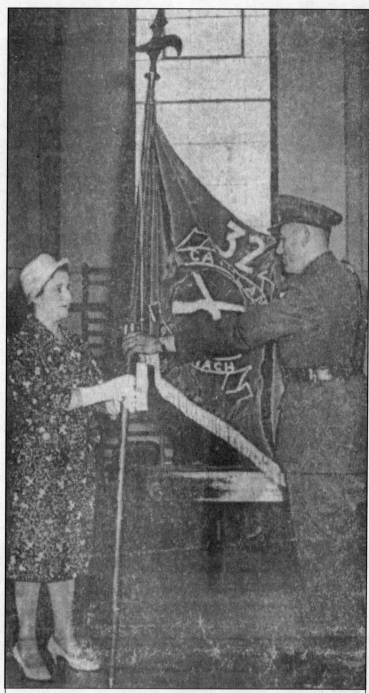

*During the ceremony at the Curragh Camp a special flag was
presented by the women of the Camp to Lt. Col. Buckley.*

A FLIGHT INTO THE UNKNOWN

From Michael O'Halloran
EVENING PRESS Staff Reporter

IT is just 3 a.m. here at Leopoldville airport and in a few minutes I shall be boarding a United Nations plane to make the 1,000-mile flight to Goma to await the arrival there of the Irish battalion.

Travelling with me are Irish headquarters officers, who have been working against the clock to prepare the way for the battalion's arrival. Their task now is to assess the situation and set up battalion H.Q. in Bukavu, south of Lake Kivu, 100 miles from Goma. A company will be sent to Kindu, 500 miles to the east, and a second plane will shortly leave for there.

We are flying into the unknown. United Nations staff here can only surmise what the situation in the mountainous Kivu province is likely to be. Last reports said the situation was "calm but tense," but so far there is no reason to believe that our men will be going into immediate danger.

Our plane is the first U.N. aircraft to make the flight to this part of the country and the Irish officers and N.C.O.s have an important and, possibly, delicate task ahead of them. As the first U.N. representatives in the region they will have to make a rapid survey of the situation and report back to Leopoldville, as well as preparing the local population for the arrival of a battalion of white troops.

Near Katanga

The Irish troops will be based only about 200 miles from the possible No. 1 trouble spot—Katanga province—and may be the first U.N. troops to enter the province, should the situation require it.

The job of establishing a staff headquarters in contact with outlying parts of the province will be a difficult one because of the poor communications network. Thirty-man units will be ranged over the entire region and some form of at least intermittent communications must be maintained with these.

A great deal of initiative will be left to the unit commanders and in these completely alien circumstances this will be a great test of their ability. However, U.N. staff are confident the battalion's mission will be efficiently carried out.

Much cooler

As I write, my plane is revving up outside in the black African night. It is now much cooler than the sticky humidity we experienced here during the day, and it is pleasant to learn that Kivu province has a climate which is not unlike that of European Mediterranean countries.

We will be just below the Equator but the high altitudes of the region keep the temperatures within reasonable limits.

Before the emergency there were some 14,000 whites in Kivu—a coffee growing centre — including about 4,500 in Bukavu. Many of these, however, are thought to have gone into Tanganyika and Uganda when the troubles began and it is not known how many have returned.

[Evening Press, Thursday, 28 July 1960]

Lt. Col. Mortimer Buckley, O.C. 32nd Battalion.

First troops forming the 32nd. Battalion arriving in the Curragh Military Camp.

Chapter 2

Departure Day

At 8.45am on Wednesday morning, 27 July 1960, the history making Irish troops departed the Curragh Military Camp, and a large convoy of trucks brought them to Dublin Castle. Here they formed up in preparation for a ceremonial parade through the streets of Dublin, prior to the airlift to the Congo later that day.

Heading up the column was the brass band of the Southern Command. The UN Battalion's own pipe band fell in behind them. Next to take up position was the National Flag colour party and, behind them, Lieutenant Edward Cassidy proudly bore the new battalion's very own flag. The staff officers group was led by Lt. Col. Mortimer Buckley, Commanding Officer of the 32nd Battalion, Very Rev. Fr. Cyril Crean, the Head Chaplain to the Forces, and his assistant, Rev. Fr. Gregory Brophy.

Headquarters Company was led by their Commanding Officer Capt. P. Reidy, followed by "A" Company from Eastern Command, with Comdt. D. Hassey at their head. Then came the Irish-speaking Battalion "C" Company from Galway and Athlone, led by Comdt. P. Carroll.

As the troops were forming-up in the Castle yard a loud cheer heralded the arrival of the Taoiseach, Sean Lemass, at the G.P.O. in O'Connell Street. He was greeted by a salute from the Number One Army Band. He then inspected a guard of honour drawn from the 2nd Motor Squadron, Dublin, under Lieut. C. O'Rourke.

Parade

The column swung out through the Castle gates at 11am en route to O'Connell Street. One of the biggest crowds ever to watch a military parade in Ireland had gathered. The tens of thousands of onlookers who lined the footpaths along Dame Street, Westmoreland Street and O'Connell Street waved small tri-colours, handkerchiefs and scarves and cheered their Army as they marched smartly past. Shop, office, hotel and restaurant staff in the centre of the city abandoned

their duties, and motorists their cars, to crowd onto the streets and join with everybody else who had come to bid farewell to the Congo bound peace makers.

A platform stretching the length of the central facade of the G.P.O. was erected to accommodate members of the Government, the Lord Mayor Cllr. Maurice Dockrell and the Army General Staff. Opposite this saluting base, a military lorry was provided for the use of the Press. The event was recorded by BBC T.V. newsreel and press cameramen, as well as myself in my capacity as the 32nd Battalion's own newsreel cameraman. The Irish Television Station (RTE) had not yet been established.

The enthusiastic and proud citizens of Ireland who had gathered in such huge numbers, some with tears in their eyes, to salute these hand picked volunteers, made it clear to all on parade that they wished them well on their perilous mission to Africa and for a safe return home.

The parade route ended at Parnell Square and the convoy got under way again, with one half of the force going to McKee Barracks and the other to Baldonnel to attend farewell dinners.

Last parade on Irish soil

At Baldonnel Aerodrome, the entire Battalion assembled for the last parade on Irish soil. The Irish Air Corps Base (later, in 1966, to be named Casement Aerodrome) was a hive of activity as Operation Sarsfield got under way. Air Corps personnel, who at this time were low in manpower, were stretched to the limit, making all the necessary preparations for the biggest military airlift ever to happen in Ireland. Whether re-fuelling aircraft, loading stores and equipment, giving technical back-up, accommodating the American aircrews, providing security or erecting barriers for the safety of the visiting public, the men of the Air Corps carried out every task with enthusiasm, efficiency and professionalism. Relatives and friends of the troops as well as spectators were brought by a

23

special fleet of buses, provided by CIE (Coras Iompar Éireann), the national train and bus company, to witness the airlift, emphasising the historic nature of the operation. For those who could make it to Baldonnel, there was less than an hour to find and impart a final emotional farewell to their loved ones.

It was intended that I go to Baldonnel for the farewell dinner and to collect some personal items from my office there, before our departure. Immediately after the parade finished in O'Connell Street I said goodbye to my father who had stood alongside me as he filmed with my eight-millimetre movie camera.

From the elevated location on the tailboard of the army lorry I noticed Bernie in the crowd. I was delighted to see her and it gave me an unexpected final chance to kiss her goodbye. When I eventually got to Parnell Square all the military trucks had departed and, with the huge crowds in O'Connell Street, it was silly to even think of looking for my father who could have taken me out to the camp. So I walked towards O'Connell Bridge contemplating a plan of action.

Do You Want a Lift?
Suddenly an army officer approached me. Pointing to the tricolour badge on my sleeve he asked, "Are you supposed to be going to the Congo?" Explaining that I had missed the transport, he offered to take me to McKee Barracks and I gladly accepted. The meal was well under way when I got there. Although it was a good meal I can't say I enjoyed it much because I was thinking of how little time I had to organise my things.

After the meal I immediately went to my office but found it locked.

Corporal Stephen Murphy, on duty in the Orderly Room, made an announcement on the public address system for Corporal Jimmy Savage to report to the Drawing Office, which he promptly did. It was important to have the film that I had left there but I also wanted to take my trumpet with me for I knew I would miss the colourful gigs with the Airchords Showband.

Airman Gerard McKevitt came into the office as I was packing my last items. "Your father gave me this form for you to sign", he said, holding it up for me to see. Because I wanted my personal 'dark-room' equipment shipped to Africa, an insurance form required my signature. I duly signed the form, gathered my belongings and the three of us hurried to the airfield.

There, Flight Sergeant Charlie Rooney of the Air Corps Photographic Section handed me film and flash bulbs, which I had asked him to order. He then got on with his job of photographing the by now assembled first Irish United Nations Peacekeeping Force.

Archbishop's Address
Opposite the aircraft hangars a small platform was set-up, and from this the Archbishop of Dublin, Most Rev. J. C. McQuaid, blessed the troops and the aircraft. In an address to the men, the Archbishop said: "You are leaving Ireland on a mission of peace. For that reason the African people will welcome you. You will be careful not to judge the Africans by the disturbances that are happening. You will find a people that, like all

The Pipe Band at McKee Barracks.

the ordinary people of the world, are gentle and sympathetic and anxious to live in peace." His address concluded, "Till we can welcome you back to Ireland, I wish you in all your activity, the blessing of God and the strong protection of Our Lady."

The Archbishop was accompanied by the Chief of Staff, Maj.-General Sean MacEoin, Col.Willie Keane, O.C. Air Corps, the Minister for Defence, Kevin Boland, the Minister for External Affairs, Frank Aiken, Right Rev. Monsignor J. O'Regan, Chancellor of the Archdiocese and Rev. J. A. MacMahon, Archbishop's House.

Dressed in the traditional 'bull's wool' uniform of the time, and wearing webbing, backpacks, water bottle, shining boots and leggings, the troops eagerly approached the Lockheed Hercules transport aircraft of the 322nd Air Division, United States Air Force. The first man aboard was Sgt.-Major Peter O'Connor of Wexford, an all-army champion marksman. Seating along both sides of the aircraft was of the metal tube supported by strapping type, as used by Military troop carriers at the time and some used their tunics to make for a more comfortable seat. Each aircraft carried sixty men and eight thousand pounds (3,700 kilos.) of freight. With a final look at the Control Tower and aircraft hangars and Baldonnel Aerodrome in general, which had been my home from home for five years, I climbed aboard the second aircraft in line, number 019.

Lift-Off

At 3pm, the four Allison turbo-prop engines of one of the C-130 Lockheed Hercules roared into life and within minutes began to taxi out onto the concrete runways of the Irish Military Air Base. The huge crowd waved in the direction of the aircraft and those on board tried to wave back through the tiny porthole type windows. As the heavily laden C-130 lifted off, climbing towards the dull grey skies overhead, the number one Army Band played "Come back to Erin".

Within forty five minutes, all of Headquarters Company of the 32nd Battalion were winging their way aboard the first three aircraft on the first leg of the journey to darkest Africa. At this point private cars were still streaming into Casement Aerodrome to see the remaining nine aircraft depart, but the latecomers were disappointed because all further flights were cancelled owing to bad weather.

The next morning the airlift resumed and a further sixty men and equipment took off at 11.20am followed at regular intervals by the remainder, until soon everyone was on their way.

An eye-opener

Meanwhile the first group had arrived at Wheelus base in Libya, having stopped for re-fuelling earlier at Evereux Air Base in France. During the short stop at Evereux, the pipe band performed for the American airmen based there, while the rest of the Company was served coffee from a mobile canteen.

The dining facilities at Wheelus were a real eye opener and the first experience for the Irish troops of a twenty-four hour, self service military dining hall, providing a choice of menu, and catering for all ranks. There was no limit to the number of courses one could have, so it was a well fed group that were transported by bus to comfortable quarters for the night.

The next morning got under way with Fr. Crean celebrating Mass in one of the smaller canteens. This was followed by another performance by the 32nd's pipe band and a band from the Royal Irish Fusiliers, to the delight of the Americans. There was a wide range of goods available to Base personnel at what was known as the PX stores. Irish currency was converted into American Base money and purchases of postcards, cameras and beer were made. It was pleasantly warm in Libya, so some enjoyed a spot of sun bathing while others wrote postcards or just relaxed with a cool beer or two.

In the afternoon the troops were again airborne, this time *en route* for Kano airport in Nigeria. After refuelling at Kano the final leg of the journey to the Congo got under way.

"Wagons roll", the convoy about to depart.

The Battalion "mounts up" and their adventure begins.

The officers and men of the 32nd Battalion parade through O'Connell Street amid admiring crowds before embarking on their historic U.N. peacekeeping mission to the Congo in 1960.

[Evening Press, Wednesday, 27 July 1960]

BOUND FOR THE CONGO

[Evening Herald, Wednesday, 27 July 1960]

[The Irish Press, Thursday, 28 July 1960]

Sunday Review

THEY'VE KISSED THE BOYS GOODBYE

Her husband nearly didn't make it . . . he slipped and almost broke his ankle. Here Mrs. Mary Doolin, wife of Congo-bound Cpl. James Doolin, dresses 3½-year-old Patrick after his bath at their McKee Park home. The other children are (from left): Valerie (2), at basin, Pauline (5), Seamus (10) and Christopher (11).

IT'S "off to the Congo" for over 600 Army boys, with their kitbags on their shoulder (guitars, accordions inside), leaving their girls behind them as they go to help win the day.

The "girls"—wives, mothers, sisters, cousins and sweethearts—are proud of the courageous volunteers. Many of them have kissed "good-bye" already, with envy of the sunshine and the new world they are going to see "for free," and a few sentimental tears for the moving moment.

By IRENE FFRENCH

Already, in most homes, the soldier has gone. The farewells (with parties) have been enjoyed. All that remains now is the chance of another farewell kiss—at the Curragh, or McKee Barracks, where they may lunch "in transit," or Baldonnel Airport as they board the plane.

But life goes on. Children laugh and play and talk about "Daddy's gone to the Congo." Wives go shopping and cooking and ironing, and have already started counting the days till the man of the house comes home again.

Exciting week

For Corporal Liam Beecher (24), of the Signal Corps, it has been an exciting week. A bachelor, who lives with his ex-Army Sergeant father and his mother in McKee Park, his "Mum" sat up long hours stitching ribbons on to the uniform he will wear till he gets his tropical kit.

"I was up all hours getting him ready," says Mrs. Mary Beecher. "This is almost his first trip abroad, although he has been once to Lourdes."

In the home of Corporal James Doolin, also at McKee Park, life was very much as usual yesterday afternoon. Mrs. Mary Doolin was busily bathing the smallest of their six children in a bathtub on the kitchen table.

Patrick (3½) was the "victim" when I called. His sister Valerie was interested in "the Congo, the Congo."

Playing around the room and looking as happy as any children can be were Christopher (11), Seamus (10), Pauline (5), and one-month-old Margaret snoozing in her pram.

Fit again

Mrs. Doolin told me: "James almost didn't go at all. He went to say good-bye to some relations and slipped on the way home and nearly broke his ankle.

"But the Army doctor has passed him as fit now, although he pulled a muscle."

Another busy home is that of Private Thomas Wolfe, where his Kilkenny-born wife, Alice, is happily looking after their six children.

"Party?" she laughed. "We hadn't time. He only had a few hours notice to get ready and leave and by the time he had gone around to visit his five brothers and four sisters, and our 2-year-old son Joseph, who has been in hospital 12 months, it was time to say good-bye."

Yesterday evening, Mrs. Wolfe was telling her children—Michael (9), Anne (5), Catherine (4), Margaret (3) and Thomas (3 months and more interested in his bottle) all about the Congo.

In the corner of the Wolfe's living-room is a knitting machine. "Tom won't need any sweaters to

"A terrible shock when he told me he was going," said Mrs. Alice Hendrick, of Quinn's Lane. In the photograph with her is two-year-old daughter Linda.

"I feel everyone should see as much of the world as they can," says Mrs. Annie Webster, of 12 Clonfert road, Kimmage.

Private Webster, however, may not be able to say farewell to his son Michael (5), on holiday with his grandmother in Arklow at present.

But in Dublin, his second son, Gerald (1 year, 8 months), is waiting to wave "bye" to his father at Baldonnel.

'Sweet sorrow'

For childhood sweethearts Mrs. Annie Hendrick (22) and her husband James (also 22), a Private for the last year and three months, "parting is sweet sorrow."

"It was such a terrible shock when he told me he was going," she said, "I had to sit down, I couldn't stand up. I suppose I'll get over it, but at present I feel just miserable.

"We met when I was 12 and we

[Sunday Review, 24 July 1960]

29

THE CONGO 1960 – The First Irish UN Peacekeepers

Little William O'Connor being lifted by his mother to receive a farewell hug from his father, as he embarked on the Congo mission.

Airborne Volunteers For The Congo

[Irish Independent, Thursday, 28 July 1960]

"Operation Sarsfield" Is Under Way
IRISH TROOPS FLY OUT
WEATHER HALTS NINE AIRCRAFT

Ireland's biggest military airlift, "Operation Sarsfield", began yesterday afternoon when three special flights of Lockheed Hercules transports of the 322nd Air Division, United States Air Force, took some of Ireland's "Congo Army" on the first stage of its flight to the Congo Republic.

The remaining nine flights last night were cancelled owing to bad weather, and will, conditions permitting, be resumed this morning. The airlift will be completed this evening with five further flights which will take the battalion's stores and heavy equipment.

Earlier, the Irish Battalion, led by its O/C., Lieut.-Col. Buckley, paraded through the principal streets of Dublin. The salute was taken by the Taoiseach, Mr. Lemass, at the G.P.O. Thousands lined the parade route and cheered the troops as they marched past.

[Irish Independent, Thursday, 28 July 1960]

Guard of honour being inspected by the Taoiseach, Seán Lemass, in O'Connell Street, Dublin, prior to their departure.

Most Rev. J. C. McQuaid archbishop of Dublin with Rev. Fr. C. P. Crean, Senior Chaplain, 32nd Battalion.

Military Chaplains.

Aboard at last and the ordeal of farewell over, soldiers make themselves comfortable for the trip that will take them to the heart of Africa.

[The Irish Press, Thursday, 28 July 1960]

Dancing with Paul Jones

Trumpet in the Congo

The Airchords Showband — Lost a trumpeter to the Congo.

OPERATION SARSFIELD which has affected so many people in this country, has also left its mark on the Baldonnel Bandwaggon.

Among the many thousands gathered to give a rousing send-off to the 32nd Battalion U.N.E.F. were the members of the newly-formed Airchords Showband from Baldonnel.

They were there because boarding one of the many "flying boxcars" was Archie Raeside, trumpeter with the Airchords and one of the 689

Irish soldiers who will be policing the Congo troublespot.

Archie goes out as one of the aeronautical section and in addition to his duties as a member of the friendly force will replace his trumpet with the gear of a photographer. We wish him well and a safe return to his trumpeting with the Airchords.

[Evening Press, Friday, 29 July 1960]

My friends Jimmy Savage, Mella Rodgers and Babs Keegan of Air Corps Headquarters staff come to say farewell.

Enjoying a cool drink.

Writing home begins at Wheelus Air Base.

Many were missing their families already

Having a break during a refuelling stop. The author is the soldier without the cap.

At Wheelus Air Base.
(Left to right): Lt. H. Daly, Assistant Adjutant 32nd Battalion, a Royal Irish Fusiliers Officer; Lt. Col. M. Buckley O.C. 32nd Battalion; Rev. Fr. C. P. Crean, Senior Chaplain 32nd Battalion.

Chapter 3

Goma – Day One

Dawn was breaking in Goma on Friday 29th July as the first Irish troops came to town. Of the initial three aircraft to leave Baldonnel just two made it on schedule. The third Hercules C-130 experienced some mechanical problems and was forced to remain in Libya overnight. It arrived the following day, albeit with only three engines running.

Originally it was intended to stop over at Leopoldville, but because of unrest in the Kivu province the battalion was re-routed directly to Goma. The pilots showed much skill when making landing look easy on the town's solitary runway, a relatively short tarmacadam strip built during World War II.

Large crowds

We were very surprised at the huge numbers of local people gathered to witness the arrival of the Irish, particularly at such an early hour, and the troops were somewhat apprehensive as to what type of a welcome they would receive. A stroke of genius from Lt. Col. Buckley put everyone at ease. He decided to form up the Pipe Band and have them perform for the crowd as the troops exited the aircraft.

Led by orange coloured kilted pipers and drummers, the Irish Army brought broad smiles to the faces of the onlookers, and very quickly the Congolese were clapping their hands and dancing to the music. Tension on both sides vanished and the newcomers were greeted with shouts of 'jambo' from all sides. This was the first Swahili word the Irish were to hear, but they would learn many more, with the help of a small phrase book, to sufficiently master this unfamiliar language in order to effectively carry out their duties as peacekeepers.

Culture shock

The coolness of the early morning air was something we had not expected, and the heavy 'bulls' wool' uniforms, designed for the home climate, were appreciated. Remember, in the Ireland of 1960, foreign

---

IRISHMEN LAND AT GOMA

Task to secure airfields

From RAYMOND SMITH
Herald Staff Reporter

Leopoldville

TO-DAY WHERE, IT WAS EARLIER REPORTED, SOME OF THE FOOD SUPPLIES WHICH HAD ARRIVED IN ADVANCE FOR THE IRISH FORCE HAD BEEN SEIZED. THE INCIDENT, HOWEVER, IS NOW OFFICIALLY DESCRIBED AS BEING OF A MINOR NATURE.

The first plane landed at 6 29 a.m. (Irish time) and the second touched down seven minutes later. The U.N. authorities hope to have all 18 planes of the Irish airlift at Goma by to-morrow.

The remaining 16 planes are at Tripoli and on their way from there to Leopoldville, they will stop off at Karo in Nigeria for refuelling.

Goma is one of the centres where the 32nd Irish Battalion will be operating. Their main task will be to gain control of three airports — at Goma, Bukavu and Kindu — for the United Nations. There are 2,000 members of the Force Publique in the province.

Commandeered

Reports reaching Leopoldville state that the first plane to land at Goma yesterday, was encircled by members of the Force Publique, whose green uniforms are somewhat similar in colour to our own Army uniform. The rations in the plane are understood to have been commandeered on the spot.

The second aircraft is believed to have touched down at an airfield in the Kivu Province and

as far as my information goes it was unmolested.

I understand that General Von Horn, the Swedish Commander of the U.N. Forces, will probably fly to Kivu Province to get a true picture of the confused situation there.

I am typing this dispatch in the cold of the early morning, just before I leave Leopoldville by air for the Kivu country where the main body of Irish troops of the U.N. forces in the Congo are stationed.

Our troops are fortunate to have been assigned to a region which has the most temperate climate of the vast Congo and also the most breathtaking scenery.

I have met people in Leopoldville who have been on safari to the Kivu country, where there is no scarcity of elephants, lions and buffalos.

Congo Irish

I have met quite a number of interesting Irish people since coming to Leopoldville.

How Miss Joy Kidd of Westport, Co. Mayo, came to be in the capital of the Belgian Congo co-operating with the U.N. staff makes a story in itself.

Miss Kidd, who is at present attached to the World Health Organisation, worked with the International Refugee Organisation in Geneva from 1948-1951 and then transferred to the Food and Agricultural Organisation in Rome.

She also went on a special mission to India for four

OUR MAN IN THE CONGO ... Staff Reporter Raymond Smith who sent us this on-the-spot story from Leopoldville to-day.

IRISH RED CROSS TO SEND TEAM TO THE CONGO

Herald Staff Reporter

The Irish Red Cross Society is to send a team to the Congo, it was announced in

the League of Red Cross Societies launched in Geneva to-day the appeal for hospitals in the Congo. According

[Evening Herald, Friday, 29 July 1960]

holidays were an alien concept to most people and the vast majority of the men of the 32nd Battalion were no different. The smell of the African countryside, the vast areas of jungle and the throngs of excited black people in unfamiliar dress was a real culture shock.

The small advance party had made arrangements to have Congolese army trucks transport the men and equipment to their new home. This was an experience in itself but the men had been forewarned. Item seven of a short leaflet titled 'some hints on the Congo', which was issued before leaving Ireland, stated that the Congolese drove very fast. They certainly did. The trucks raced away from the airport along dirt roads in a cloud of dust, throwing the occupants, twenty per truck, about with every turn and bump in the road, of which there were many.

Our First Barracks in Africa

Our new home was in a primary school and college located a few miles outside the now deserted Goma town. This became the Irish army's first barracks in Africa. The two complexes were located opposite each other, with the road from the south separating them. A surprising feature was the non-existence of any form of boundary wall or fence to enclose either of the institutions, in contrast with similar groups of buildings back home. As soon as everyone had a bed space secured, the first of the United Nations personal kit was issued. This consisted of two pairs of lightweight slacks (combats), two khaki shirts, a blue helmet and mosquito repellent. Dressed in the new tropical uniforms, the battalion formed up for inspection before parading out of camp.

First parade

This first parade on African soil was to a small mission church on a hill, about a mile from camp and was proudly led by the chaplain, Fr. Crean. To the local people this was a great spectacle and they clapped and danced as they followed the marching ranks of soldiers, adding a carnival atmosphere to the occasion. There were no seats in the church, which was just as well, for it meant the building could accommodate both the Irish peacekeepers and their new neighbours. Fr. Crean celebrated the Mass in Latin, as was the custom of the day and was familiar to the locals. The Latin Mass was something we had in common and it helped in the shaping of good relationships. The return to camp was greeted just as enthusiastically by the locals as was the outward march.

Priorities

There was a great deal to be done on our first day in Africa. Priorities were to secure the base and set up checkpoints in the locality as well as on the immediate border with Rwanda. The Corps of Engineers set up generators and emergency water-supply tanks and pumps. Although there was no possibility of communications with Ireland, the Signals Corps organised their equipment to maintain voice contact with patrols at medium range, and Morse code would be used for greater distances. As described later, there was to be an improvement in communications with Ireland, courtesy of ham (amateur) radio.

As soon as Dr. Laffan and the 'medics' got organised in setting up a clinic, they had a constant flow of patients from the local community. The service was so popular that the numbers attending the daily clinic reached 150. This depleted the medical supplies, and it became clear that the manpower was not available to attend to the Battalion's needs and look after the civilian population as well. Following a United Nations directive forbidding aid of this nature, the service was withdrawn.

A civilian West German Red Cross team arrived soon after and patients were redirected there. Some still preferred to come to the Battalion clinic because there was a charge of 5 francs at the Government hospital. The Congolese excluded members of other tribes, particularly Watutsis, from attending the Red Cross clinics, so some continued to seek medical aid from the Irish.

Workstations were established by the tailor, shoemaker, artificer and all the other support groups necessary to keep an army on the move. The catering personnel familiarised themselves with the kitchen equipment in the college and were soon in the position of providing three square meals a day to our troops. Was it Napoleon who said, 'an army marches on its stomach'?

End of a long day

At the end of what was a long and extremely busy day, the majority of those who had arrived at Goma on the first three aircraft finally got to bed, but with advice to stay alert and preferably not to remove their boots. For some, sleep would have to be delayed because guards had to be posted around the camp and the surrounding area. During the night, the duty officer, Comdt. J. Adams visited the checkpoints for their reports. While he was in discussion with one guard commander at a post on the Rwanda border, the stillness of the night was shattered by a loud explosion. He shone a flashlight on his helmet to indicate to whoever fired the grenade that he was United Nations personnel, and then proceeded across the border into Rwanda. Confronting a group of Belgian paratroopers, they admitted responsibility for the incident, which they claimed was an accident.

It could be said that the first night for the Irish in Africa went off with a bang!

Congolese troops supply the only transport available.

Cpl. Michael ('the Hike') Kavanagh distributes biscuits to young helpers.

Capt. P. Reidy briefing his Military Police section prior to a mission.

The Pipe Band appreciate their much lighter tropical uniform.

Stepping out on our first Church Parade in Africa.

Excited local people follow the parade.

Preparing sandwiches at Goma.

Portable canvas water tanks are filled by the engineers.

The shoemaker at work.

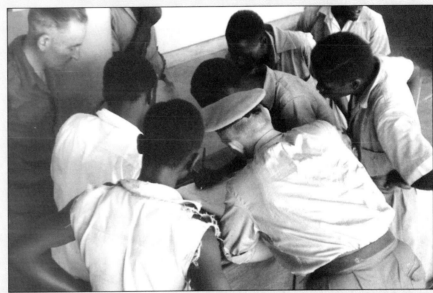

Local labour being paid.

Empty crates are the tailor's work bench.

Dan Shine is one of the cooks at work in the college kitchen.

A dining marquee being erected.

Building a barbed wire enclosure.

Local people patiently await medical aid from the Irish.

Border checkpoints are established.

*Irish and Belgian troops meet on the border with Rwanda.
(Left to right): Belgian Paratrooper, Sgt. T. Dowse, Belgian Paratrooper, Capt. P. Reidy, next man unidentified, Sgt. D. Bennett, back row Cpl. C. Heavey.*

REPORT ON THE CONGO FROM O'HALLORAN

YESTERDAY green-clad troops of the 32nd Battalion U.N.E.F. in the Congo took over patrol duty in the Goma district of the Kivu province of the troubled Congo. This was the result of the agreement negotiated by their commander, Lt-Col. Mortimer Buckley.

The members of the mutinous Force Publique have agreed to carry arms only in their own camps and the Irish troops are now maintaining the peace in this section of the new state. IRISH PRESS reporter, Michael O'Halloran, sends this up-to-the-minute despatch.

Kivu President praises our troops
'IRISH ARE OUR FRIENDS

Men in green on patrol in Goma

STANDING on the tarmac of the little airport here before his 'plane took off for Bukavu, Mr. Nihuru, sident of the Kivu Province, spoke highly in praise he Irish troops and expressed his pleasure at the lt of the talks which he had just concluded with Lt.

[The Irish Press, Tuesday, 2 August 1960]

Our own transport begins to arrive.

Chapter 4

Confidence Building

On Saturday, 30 July 1960, we woke up to our first dawn under Congolese skies. Back home it was a bank holiday weekend but for the men of the 32nd Battalion it was work as usual. We knew that we would be 'on call' twenty-four hours a day for the next six months.

Aircraft continued to arrive from Ireland throughout the day, and the Battalion numbers grew. The local people had never seen the road from the airport so busy, as Congolese Army trucks ferried men and equipment to the base camp. A few (old) Irish registered Landrovers and some new UN Jeeps arrived by air in the following days, allowing a greater degree of mobility. Some Congolese Army lorries were sprayed white (well nearly white) by our engineers at an abandoned local garage, and kept on semi-permanent loan for our own use.

The Bishop of Goma, Monsignor Busimba, arrived at the camp next day to welcome the Irish to the area and was invited to return the following Friday for an official visit. A guard of honour was assembled to greet him the following week when he was accompanied by a number of Missionary Fathers.

Irish in control

The appeal by President Joseph Kasavubu and Prime Minister Patrice Lumumba to the UN to remove all Belgian and other foreign troops from the entire Congo seemed to work well in the Kivu Province. Within a remarkably short time the Irish were very much in control of the region. Some of the local armed forces were in disarray having been stripped of their officer corps, who formerly consisted of white Belgians. Now their leaders were fellow Congolese, drawn from serving non-commissioned officers (NCOs), who did not command the same authority as the Belgian officers. Lt. Col. Buckley was successful in reaching agreement with Mr. Nihuru, President of Kivu Province, Mr. Midiburu, Vice President, and Col. Six, commanding officer of troops in the area, "that

their forces would not carry weapons outside their camp".

Good tactic

Even with this agreement in place, there were rebel troops roaming the countryside. Indeed on the first Monday under Irish control, a group of rebel troops armed with automatic rifles came out from the cover of the bush on the western side of Goma airport. Their intention was to take control of this vital link with the rest of the Congo. The airport guard of the 32nd Battalion had no intention of allowing this to happen and immediately took up defensive positions. The UN orders were not to open fire unless fired upon, so there was tension in the air as hand grenades were primed just in case. One young Irish soldier was 'stood down' for prematurely loading his rifle before being ordered to do so.

The defensive actions of the Irish were sufficient to deter the advancing soldiers and they withdrew back to the cover of the bush. The stalemate was resolved when an Irish Landrover, with a Vickers machine gun mounted in the back, approached the rebel troops patrolling the perimeter of the runway. A second Landrover with 'C' rations (emergency food) was positioned within sight of the hiding soldiers and the armed vehicle returned to the airport building. The tactic was a good one because it showed that the U.N. would not surrender control of the airport, but by providing food was a friend of the Congolese people. The message was understood and within a short period the rebel troops withdrew, each with a food parcel under his arm.

It was vital to control the airport as this was the main route by which mail and supplies were received and troops dispatched to other areas. Travelling by boat was another option but this was a much slower means of transport. Indeed that same day a group from 'A' company was supposed to fly out to Kindu but, with the expected aircraft not arriving, they proceeded by boat to Bukavu along Lake Kivu.

Settling in
Within a few days we were settling into a routine of sorts, which could be disrupted at any given moment. As professional soldiers, everyone was prepared to accept whatever duty was required at the time or carry out any new orders without question. As the official photographer I kept myself in readiness to record the activities of the Battalion as they occurred. Taking photographs and filming events at the airport as well as accompanying patrols and escorts of long and short duration kept me busy. Although there was no 'clocking-out' time, as such, for those of us not detailed for a specific duty the evenings were generally considered to be our own time. This could be spent writing home, playing cards or just chatting. I did all of these and also on occasions played a few tunes on the trumpet as well. One evening I was approached by some NCO.s from the medical section and I was asked if I would like to join them for a walk.

The 'village hop'
We left the camp and headed in the direction of Goma town. We had no particular plan in mind and enjoyed the walk and idle gossip. After perhaps half an hour we heard singing and music to our left, so we stopped walking and listened. The sound was coming from a cluster of low buildings some distance from the road. After a short discussion we decided to investigate. On approaching what was the native village of Goma, we continued on past a number of traditional African hut style dwellings and headed for a larger single storey but much more substantial building, which we took to be the 'community hall'.

A young Congolese Army Lieutenant greeted us warmly and invited us inside. It seemed the whole village were in celebratory mode as men and women danced to the rhythm of what sounded like rock music. As a founder member of the Airchords Showband, I was interested in the line-up of the local dance band. They consisted of a vocalist, a couple of drummers, guitarist and an instrumentalist. As to what the latter was playing, I have no idea. His instrument appeared to be a stick pulled into a curved shape by string or, perhaps, catgut. It was held in a similar fashion to a violin and, by drawing a bow across the string, various notes could be created. The drums were in fact 'tom-toms'. Two of them were familiar upright types and another was a hollow tree-trunk about a meter and a half long and laid horizontally. I was impressed with the tones the drummer could produce by working the 'drumsticks' along this strange drum. The instrumentalists provided the rhythm while the singer provided

what melody there was. The combination was like nothing I had ever seen or heard before and I was thrilled to witness genuine central African entertainment. The dancers gyrated to the music, not unlike the popular 60's rock and roll back home.

Joined in
I was content to observe and listen but the young officer obviously thought we might like to join in and introduced us to dancing partners. Having been advised by no less than the Archbishop of Dublin, Dr. McQuaid, during his farewell address at Baldonnel, to treat the Congolese as friends and not wishing to give offence, we joined in.

In Ireland at that time, refreshments at a dance consisted of a mineral bar and, when a girl was invited to join in a drink, it meant a glass of lemonade or orange and, in some dance halls, it was even possible to get a cup of coffee. We soon learned that things were a little different in the Congo at the 'village hop', where bottles of Simba (the local beer) were consumed as one danced. We entered into the spirit of the occasion and were getting along fine until someone in our group was advised that Irish Military Police were approaching. Unsure whether we should be at the dance or not and not wishing to cause anyone embarrassment – not to mention the possibility of being considered AWOL (absent without official leave) – we decided to leave.

There was a curtained opening in the wall behind the band and we were ushered through this by our Congolese friend. As we stepped out into the darkness of the night we found our way around the village huts, guided only by the light of the moon until we reached the road. As we headed back to camp with a spring in our step and the native music fading in the distance, it was unanimously agreed that, certainly, it had been a more interesting evening than playing cards.

The bees
On a routine local area patrol with Captain P. Reidy, Sargent D. Bennett and Corporal Christy Heavey, we decided to drive to the top of Mount Goma where we would get a good view of the area. The road, more like a track, was narrow and winding and on some sharp bends, the wheels of the jeep spun on the loose surface as they tried to get a grip. Most roads we encountered were much as one would expect in Central Africa but, as Mount Goma was an extinct volcano, it was almost surprising that there was a route, which could take any vehicle. On reaching the summit we left the jeep and stood silently in awe of the magnificent view to the west, where the vast plains stretched out as far as the eye could see. Nyiragongo, an active volcano to the north, somehow seemed a lot closer when viewed from here rather than from our base camp. Westward

*Monsignor Busimba and his clergy
with officers of the 32nd. Battalion.*

*Monsignor Busimba, Bishop of Goma
with Comdt. P. O'Carroll and
Rev. Fr. C. P. Crean.*

*Lt. Col. M. Buckley following
negotiations with local officials.*

across the border in Ruanda, Karasimbi towered 1000ft above us at 4500ft.

Corporal Heavey interrupted our thoughts. He pointed to a dark cloud in the distance and, although there was no wind, it appeared to be moving towards us. As it came closer we became aware of a humming sound and realised the noise was coming from the cloud. "It's a swarm of bees!" someone called out in a voice tinged with alarm and we made a dash for the jeep. We had been warned of some of the possible dangers from various sources in this unfamiliar land and no one was prepared to wait around to check this one out. 'Stung to death' was not what I wanted on my service record. As we reached the vehicle it was clear the droning swarm of bees was heading straight for us and getting closer. Somehow there seemed to be a lot more twists in the narrow track as we raced down the side of the volcano, enveloped in a cloud of dust. Back safely at our camp we felt fortunate not to have been enveloped in that cloud of bees.

Maintaining good relations

Sensitive to the suffering of the people of the Congo while not being there in a humanitarian aid role, the Irish soldiers provided what help they could from their own supplies and rations. Maintaining good relations with the local forces was a key element of Irish policy, and in keeping with this, the pipe band responded to an invitation to play at their camp. Led around their base by the Irish pipers, the Congolese soldiers marched smartly, in step and in time to the music. It was clear to see that they were very proud when Comdt. Bill O'Carroll complimented them on their smart and soldierly turnout.

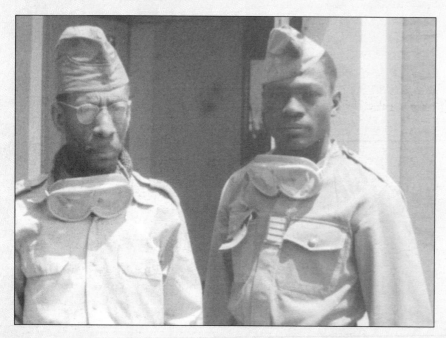

Colonel Six from the local Congolese forces and his Sgt. Major.

At Goma Port on Lake Kivu.

*On deck and about to sail for Bukavu,
left to right: "Forty" O'Brien,
Charlie Robinson and Pte. Finlay.*

Writing up my diary.

*Child goat-herders. Our camp is in the
background.*

Local children are never far from our camp.

"Room Service" as one of the lads provides a cup of tea. The wooden crate is the boy's home.

Smoking fish over an open fire at a Goma village.

Native quarters at Goma.

Off duty in the sun at Goma.
L to R.: Cpl. Heavey (MPC), Sgt. P. Dignam, (at the rear, the next 3 are unidentified), BQMS. P. Harrington,
CQMS. D. Nolan, CQMS. K. Mc.Court and a young visitor wearing a specimen of the local fauna on his head.

At the top of Mount Goma. (L. to R.): The author, Sgt. D. Bennett and Capt. P. Reidy.

The Congolese army parade out of their camp without weapons.

Our Pipe Band leading Congolese parade.

FRI. 5TH AUG '60

After Mass, the first thing I done was clean my cameras after yesterdays dusty trip. I then took some pictures of the shoe maker and the tailor at work. The natives employed by the 32nd; to work around the camp buildings were being paid to-day, so I got some snaps of them receiving their cash.

The Bishop of Goma Monseigneur Busimba, came to the camp and I filmed him inspecting the guard of honour. Immediately after this, John Ross questioned me about my job and recorded the conversation for Radio Eireann.

SAT. 6TH AUG.'60

This morning, with the head chaplain to the forces, Fr. Crean, I left Goma to travel to Bukavu by road. On drawing near a small village, which we could see in the valley below the road – we noticed some children standing on the side of the road. The Padre stopped the Landrover, so that he could take some pictures of the youngsters, but just as he had them nicely arranged, one of the boys stepped from the jeep carrying his gustaff and the children ran back down the valley to their homes.

After approxamitely three hours driving we stopped to have "a 'cuppa & a cana". The sceenary around this part of the province was exquisit; it was around here that Stanley once explored.

Extracts from the Author's Diary.

Chapter 5

Branching Out

Within a week of their arrival in the Congo, the Battalion had established itself in the Goma area and well beyond. Regions such as Bukavu, Kindu, Kamina and Kasongo were also secured. Each of these sub-bases was approximately a hundred miles apart, and the tentacles of the Irish peacekeepers extended even further as mobile patrols also operated from each newly established posting.

At noon, on 4 August, I accompanied a reconnaissance patrol from Goma camp to investigate reports of terrorists operating in the Masisi area, fifty miles to the northwest. Over paved roads fifty miles is a relatively short trip but in Africa the roads are narrow, bumpy, full of potholes and extremely dusty. This particular journey took over three hours.

Halting at Masisi, we were cautiously approached by a sizeable number of frightened locals. While maintaining caution, warm and friendly greetings were extended to the growing assembly by the members of the patrol. Smiles were shared and cigarettes too, and simple words of friendship were uttered in the most basic Swahili. Captain Black went into conference with the headman of the village, a local administrator called Mr. Janvai, and some of his colleagues.

Great amusement

Satisfied that the situation was peaceful in Masisi, we began the return journey. After some time one of the truck engines overheated and we stopped to avoid causing extra damage. The patrol divided into groups and scurried into the jungle in different directions in search of water. There was great amusement when one of the groups returned very quickly, not just with the water, but also with large bunches of bananas!

This was a new experience as the only place we had seen bananas previously was in a shop. With the engine sufficiently cooled, the patrol moved on. Within another hour steam was once again hissing out of the radiator. Darkness had descended at this stage and the armed five-man team was more alert and

cautious as they left the relative security of their comrades and the only road for many miles to enter the jungle once more for water. There was little thought for banana gathering on this occasion, but they were successful in their mission and the patrol moved on. Eleven hours after setting out from Goma we arrived back at base tired, hungry and covered in a film of dust.

This was a typical routine patrol but generally the discomfort endured took a secondary role to the thrill of adventure and the experience of meeting people from many different tribes in unfamiliar territory.

Building new roads

It was important for the UN to be seen to be patrolling the region, because it helped to establish a sense of security for the local population and also served to deter rebels and feuding tribes from engaging in violence. This was apparent as people returned to their normal daily routine. Women did most of the hard work such as carrying large bundles on their heads or backs, as well as child-rearing, fetching water, cooking and all that goes with the care of one's family. They also worked in the fields at coffee plantations and planted grass at the airport. The men, on the other hand, retired to the village to play cards and quench their thirst with the local brew 'Simba'.

Some young men did exert themselves and one of the projects in progress near Goma, in which males were involved, was the building of a new road. Apart from some extinct volcanoes and an active one called Nyiragongo, which was north of our camp, the terrain generally was flat which meant the roads could run straight for long stretches. Firstly a way was cleared through the jungle and scrubland by means of controlled burning and large tree stumps were rooted out. With an abundance of lava rock deposited over huge areas for many centuries, this was the material used for the road base. Using heavy pointed steel bars and sledgehammers the rock was broken into small pieces and deposited into hollows or depressions along the route.

(Nyiragongo grabbed the attention of the world in 2002 when it again erupted. Readers will recall the television pictures showing apocalyptical scenes of devastation and destruction. Practically the entire town of Goma was buried beneath the hot molten rock.)

A visit to Bukavu

It was four days since 'A' Company had relocated to Bukavu and the Padre, Father Cyril Crean, was anxious to visit them at their new location. When groups of men were posted to other areas, it was important for purposes of morale to let them know that they were not forgotten about, either by their former comrades or by those at headquarters. This was particularly important in the Congo, as communications could be very poor, bordering on non-existent for long periods in some areas. Visits by headquarters staff and other United Nation's dignitaries or medical teams provided the link necessary to alleviate feelings of isolation and it also served to keep the men vigilant and alert at all times.

I accompanied Father Crean on this particular trip to Bukavu, along with an armed party of eight. We travelled in two Landrover jeeps. More than an hour into the journey, as the convoy reached higher ground, we could see a small village in the distance ahead. Fr. Crean noticed a group of children standing at the side of the road and asked for the patrol to stop. As they stood quietly observing the white strangers there was fear in the childrens' eyes. Some of them had swollen bellies, thin arms and legs, and were clearly suffering from malnutrition.

Father Crean approached them unhurriedly, putting them at immediate ease, and soon they were smiling and lining up to have a group photograph taken. But the photo opportunity was ruined when a member of our escort unwittingly ambled towards the kids, causing them to scatter into the jungle. The effect that seeing an armed soldier had on them was clear and, despite reassuring calls from our group, they wouldn't come back. Who could tell what scenes of violence they had witnessed in their country's recent turbulence.

A couple of hours later our escort halted for a cup of tea and a sandwich. The beauty of the countryside around us was overwhelming and impossible not to admire. It was plain to see just why non-Africans would want to settle here.

A little later we were met at a place called Kalehe by the patrol from Bukavu, which consisted of Lt. Enright, two NCO's, and three men. This patrol would accompany us for the completion of the jour-

ney, allowing the other patrol to return to their base at Goma. Since it was now 11.30am and the patrol from Bukavu had been on the road since 5.15am, Father Crean and I knew that we still had six hours of driving ahead of us. Following greetings and a short exchange of the recent news, the escorts parted and headed off to their respective base camps in opposite directions.

Seated comfortably in a Bel-Air coupe, driven by a Swedish U.N. officer, Father Crean and I relaxed and enjoyed the unfolding beauty. The driver had lived for some time in the area and was in a position to give a knowledgeable commentary as we drove through locations of particular note.

Heavy demand on men and transport

The advance party from 'A' Company had arrived in Bukavu, the capital of the Kivu province, on 1st August and consisted of five officers and twenty-seven other ranks. A Swedish interpreter was also allotted to the company. The President of the Province, Mr. Mirohu, and the local military commandant welcomed them and they quickly established control in the area, which is about a hundred miles south of Goma. Being the capital it was a much larger and more developed town than Goma. The college, which was occupied by the troops as their barracks, was appropriately larger too and very comfortable.

There was a swimming pool within a few hundred yards of the complex, complete with diving boards, dressing rooms, brightly coloured benches and even sunshades. In off duty hours this was a welcome asset because, unlike the crisp mountain air in Goma, the heat in Bukavu was more exhausting. It was doubly enjoyable for us because back in the Goma area it was not recommended to swim in the lake. Dangers lurked there, like the Bilharzia snail, for instance, which can enter the body and attack the blood cells with disastrous consequences. Needless to say warnings were heeded.

The task of protecting all of the people, both black and white, and helping to restore order and calm was the same wherever the peacekeepers were stationed. In some locations, vital installations such as electrical power, broadcasting, banking, postal and medical facilities, required constant surveillance and protection. At Bukavu, relief supplies had to be delivered to more isolated locations such as the Power Station and surrounding border posts, which placed a heavy demand on both men and transport. There was considerable friction between King Kabare and the local administrator. The King wished to keep control of administration, justice, and tax collection, but this was not in the 'spirit' of the new Republic.

At Masisi.

On the Masisi patrol.

A welcome beer.

Remarkable dedication

Reports of tribal feuding, killings and attacks on white planters were investigated and involved many patrols travelling long distances. Some patrols were away from base for many days at a time, camping out in unfamiliar and uncomfortable surroundings. A patrol typically consisted of one officer, two NCOs and six men but often it would be just half this strength. With no formal training in jungle survival, the level of dedication to duty and endurance shown by the first Irish overseas troops was, in hindsight, remarkable.

Typical reports in the company log might read as follows:

> 09.40 hours, 8th August: Patrol consisting of Captain Cantrell, two NCOs, six Privates, and one interpreter left for Kamatuka. Patrol interviewed local administrator at Mwenga and found no disturbances. Patrol then, accompanied by administrator, left for Kamituga and found no disturbances there. Patrol returned without incident at 19.30 hours, 9th August.

> 19.45 hours, 8th August: Message from Battalion HQ - "Contact civil authorities in Kalehe re attack on white planters at Kybhtz and Lutngo. Planter Jaques Van Hoegaerden". Patrol left Company HQ at 08.30 hours 9th August, i/c Lt. Wright, two NCO's, two men and Lt. Windberg - Swedish interpreter. Message proved to be correct. Worker appeared to be mishandled and one European beaten up, but not badly. Gendarme had arrested five ringleaders of trouble earlier in the day. Patrol returned 18.15 hours same day without incident.

Filming on patrol

Anxious to record as much activity as possible on film, I took every opportunity that presented itself to accompany patrols throughout the Congo. As my stay in Bukavu was a short one, it was not possible to go on extended missions there but on 8 August I did get to accompany a relief patrol. Our job was to bring supplies out to the men guarding the Central Power Station.

Following that, we took provisions to the guard at Shangugu Bridge, which spanned the border between Bukavu and Ruanda Urundi. This bridge was guarded by the UN on the Congolese side and the Belgians on the other, and was the scene of some serious conflict situations between the local police and the military. It would on occasion be closed to all movement. The conflicts arose because the airfield for Bukavu was on the Ruanda Urundi side and outside of United Nations control. I climbed a hill near the bridge and got film footage and photographs of the area and particularly of the Belgian Military Base on the far side of the river.

Boat journey

After four days of visiting outposts and ministering to the troops, it was time for Fr. Crean and myself to return to Goma. To reduce demands on the Bukavu patrol, we decided to make the return journey by boat. This would take the best part of a day, but out on the lake there was little danger from rebels or warring tribal factions.

The craft was well equipped and the passenger cabin was fitted out with comfortable seating and tables. Refreshments were available from the bar so one could sit back with a cool drink and admire the beauty of the changing landscape along the distant shores of Lake Kivu. The appearance from time to time of tropical islands, some apparently inhabited, was a surprise and it brought home the realisation of the vastness of the lake.

Some time into the journey the vessel came to a halt, dropped anchor and the engine stopped. The silence was only interrupted by the lapping of small waves against the hull. But the moment of tranquillity was shattered when a couple of blasts of the boat's whistle echoed across the lake. A dugout canoe came into view, growing ever larger as it closed on the stationary boat. When the canoe came alongside, the captain of the boat and a well-groomed boy of perhaps twelve years of age emerged from the wheelhouse. The boy, dressed in a college blazer and slacks was helped over the side from the deck of the larger craft into the raised arms of the canoe men below. With the boy seated, school satchel on his knees, the canoeists dipped and pulled rhythmically on their paddles and this ancient craft faded eastwards towards Rwanda. What a contrast to the school bus back in Ireland!

House searches

A degree of surveillance was maintained on the many abandoned houses of former white settlers in an effort to curtail wholesale looting and destruction of property. Many Europeans and, in particular, those involved in the security forces would have kept weapons in their homes. In view of the hurried evacuation of whites, there was some concern that some of these weapons might well have been left behind. To ensure that these did not end up in the wrong hands and, perhaps, be used for illegal purposes or possibly against UN troops, the houses were searched. Captain Reidy together with Sgts. Bennett and Dowse and their Military Police team found several hundreds of rounds of nine millimetre and assorted ammunition during these searches.

Engine trouble.

Precious drinking water is used to cool the engine.

School children return to their classrooms

Road building near Goma.

The author and young helper.

Nyiragongo, viewed from our camp.

The road to Bukavu.

Checking the route.

Local cattle.

Woman and baby with wood for the cooking fire.

Dublin registered Land Rover in Bukavu town.

65

Capt. Cantrell makes final checks before going on long patrol.

Border crossing.

A passenger transfers to a river taxi.

We sail past a fisherman on Lake Kivu.

Cpl. Heavey and Capt. Reidy recover ammunition in an abandoned house.

Many houses yield up live ammunition.

Chapter 6

Keeping the Peace

Lengthy discussions took place between Captain Reidy and the local Commissioner of Police, with Fr. Crean as interpreter, to inspect the prison just outside Goma town. The visit was eventually agreed to and a small group was escorted by members of Force Publique to the imposing grey stone-walled complex which was the prison. The purpose of the inspection was to ascertain if any European prisoners were being detained in custody and if so, the conditions under which they were being held. Following independence in the Congo there had been widespread anti-European demonstrations and both pro and anti-government supporters directed violence against them.

The prison governor claimed that all European prisoners had been released immediately following independence and he offered the prison register for inspection. It indicated that there were twenty-five male and three females being detained, all of them Congolese.

He then took the inspecting party on a tour of the cells and the exercise yards. In the yard there appeared to be no segregation of children from adults. Everything was very basic. Dining tables, for example, consisted of raised concrete slabs.

In the cells, the only item was the bed, if you could call it such. It consisted of rough timber planks and there was no mattress or other form of padding in evidence. They were arranged as bunks. The solitary confinement cells, which were permanently dark, had no beds at all, so by comparison the good conduct prisoners were lucky.

Some prisoners appeared to be in a poor state of health, but then so were a lot of the general public. The prison staff claimed that the women prisoners were engaged in basketry while the men were employed at trades such as book binding, woodwork, weaving and tailoring.

Negotiations with the Police Commissioner.

The Irish Military Police, with Fr.Crean and Comdt. J. Laffan visited the prison each month during their time in Goma. The regular report they submitted to ONUC Headquarters at Leopoldville apparently went mostly unheeded. Some good did come from interviewing prisoners and discussions with the Governor and his staff, however, when it was decided that young children be kept apart from adult criminals.

Education

Under Belgian rule, education of the Congolese population was seen as a threat to colonialism. Therefore it was not promoted to any degree and travelling outside of the country to be educated was also prohibited. For decades, Missionaries had established themselves in central Africa and it was these great people who provided any early formal education to the local people.

The Irish troops serving with the UN in the Congo were reminded of their own history of British colonialism and the effects that it had on Ireland. The effects of this policy could now be witnessed in a different time and in another country as it was happening. The available qualified academics required to successfully govern and administer a newly independent country, particularly one so vast, were totally inadequate. Tribalism was deliberately maintained and the cultural and dialectical differences of people in sparsely populated regions prevented the growth of any sense of nationalism.

Following independence, the distrust and hatred for 'whites' by some, spread rapidly over large areas, which was remarkable for a country with such a poor communications network. These feelings came to apply even to the missionaries who formerly were regarded as friends of the people and certainly not a threat. It was no longer safe for white priests, nuns or lay missionaries to stay in the Congo, particularly in remote areas and many left the country or moved to areas of population, where the UN was policing. Visits to three remaining Ursuline nuns to check on their welfare became a routine.

On Safari

The Irish troops sampled some of this anti-white hostility on 12 August, when a patrol reached Walikale and entered the Force Publique barracks. The patrol members were immediately ordered to surrender their arms. When this demand was refused, they were threatened with being shot immediately on suspicion of being Belgian troops in disguise. The Irish made it clear, through their interpreter, Mike Nolan, (Mike had lived in the Congo for twenty three years) that they would defend themselves and not give up without a fight. Towards morning the Congolese were finally persuaded that the patrol was in fact a United Nations

troupe and they were permitted to proceed without further incident.

The diversity of experiences continued daily in unfamiliar and volatile surroundings. Two days after the Walikale experience, by way of contrast, another patrol, of which I was part of, enjoyed the delights of what was termed a 'safari' patrol. This consisted of five officers, fourteen NCOs and other ranks, and an interpreter. The transport for the convoy consisted of two Landrovers and a Volkswagen saloon. I was excited at the prospect of experiencing the more remote and wild areas of the Congo.

This particular expedition was to go as far as a place called Rwindi and the route took the convoy through the National Albert Park. In these early days reconnaissance was important and, at the request of Captain Burke, several stops were made on the way to measure bridges and record important land features and points of reference.

Parc National Albert was amazing. Those who had visited Dublin Zoo back home had seen elephants and monkeys before, but none of us had ever seen large herds of buffalo or wild deer roaming the great plains of Africa.

A jealous hippo

Driving through wooded areas it was common to see, and hear, screaming monkeys swinging through the trees. More interesting still was the sight of numerous hippopotami wallowing in huge muddy water holes. But, for me, the best experience of all was to see the Great African elephants in their natural habitat, and to have a close encounter with them. Safari patrols were warned that elephants are fearful of humans but, if cornered or wounded, will attack and can build up to speeds of twenty miles an hour. Should elephants be encountered on the road the advice was to:

(a) stop a safe distance away,
(b) turn vehicle if possible and be ready for a getaway,
(c) close all windows,
(d) pull down flaps and secure,
(e) wait, and make no noise. Keep absolutely still. Do NOT get curious.

Late evening was a good time to view the variety of animals as they gathered to drink at their favourite watering holes in wide stretches of river. Stopping to observe this, the interpreter, who was familiar with the habits of large animals in the wild, prompted Comdt. Fleming and I to move closer to the water hole in order to get better pictures. Following instructions to approach a number of magnificent elephants from down wind, some good film was shot at about fifty

U. N. TELLS BELGIUM 'GET OUT OF CONGO'

State of emergency proclaimed

AFTER an all night session, the United Nations Security Council in New York to-day ordered Belgium to withdraw her troops "immediately" from breakaway Katanga Province, focal point of the crisis in the Congo.

But at the same time it proclaimed in effect a "hands off" policy on the Province's claim for independence. In the Congo itself, a state of emergency was proclaimed, and in Leopoldville the Government sent troops to the house of the Belgian Ambassador to insure his evacuation immediately.

[Evening Press, Tuesday, 9 August 1960]

paces. With no telephoto or zoom lens for either movie or still camera, I cautiously approached the herd. Encouraged by this success I turned the cameras on a herd of partly submerged hippos. Without warning, the muddy waters rose up like an erupting volcano and seconds later a massive bull hippo was bearing down on the pair of us. This 'would be' big game photographer beat a hasty retreat and, fortunately, the animal stopped his charge a few yards from the water's edge. Explaining that the bull was only jealous, the interpreter made light of the incident by saying that we should not have made eyes at the cows. Naturally the entire incident provided much entertainment for the members of the patrol, who were observing the scene from the safety of high ground some distance away.

A return to the old plantation

In rural areas, plantations provided much needed work for many people. As a result, small villages were established on and around these lands, which were generally owned by white people. The exodus of panic-stricken Europeans meant not only the abandonment of their homes and possessions but also their former employees. As a result a lot of workers were left unpaid when independence was declared.

One employer, a Mrs. Six, wished to redress this situation by returning to her plantation and paying her loyal workers what they were due. Accompanying a Goma patrol going in the direction of her abandoned property, this concerned and courageous lady was escorted to her former property near Ruthsura. This was located quite a distance off the main Ruthsura road and the track which led there was only as wide as one vehicle – it was worse than the worst bohreen back in Ireland. The vehicles rose and fell to the contours of the terrain as they slowly made their way along the three-mile avenue of jungle and elephant grass. Finally having endured the bumpy ride and after

fording two rivers, the enclosing vegetation gave way to a great expanse of cultivated land.

Parked in a clearing, tea was brewed and bully beef sandwiches, followed by fruit, constituted a sumptuous mid-day meal. The assembly of workers grew as word spread of our arrival. When the purpose of the visit was explained, everyone on the plantation was very happy, welcoming the patrol with broad smiles and open arms.

A large catering can of sugar was uncapped and the children enjoyed plunging their little hands into the fine sweet crystals and scooping it up. With hand to mouth and making *mmmm* sounds of satisfaction as the grains of sugar melted, each one moved aside to let the next 'sugar baby' partake in the event.

The adults of the gathered assembly were treated to a can or two of the unfamiliar taste of Guinness and the general consensus was that it was good. Leaving two military policemen with Mrs. Six while she paid the workers, and with everyone in a happy mood, the patrol moved on to its next objective.

Delivering a baby

There was a small remote hospital run by a Spanish doctor about thirty minutes drive away, and the Battalion doctor, Comdt. Laffan, was keen to visit it. Little did he know that he would be pressed into service once he arrived, for the resident doctor was about to deliver a baby and Comdt. Laffan was asked to lend a hand. The Spanish doctor said it was not common for native women to give birth in a white man's hospital, preferring their own midwife and witch doctor. This in some way explained the considerable number of anxious people gathered outside the building and the noticeable lack of in-patients.

The intention had been to proceed further on but the delay of over an hour meant that the patrol had to return immediately for Mrs. Six and escort her back to Goma before nightfall.

Capt. Reidy and Fr. Crean interview child prisoners at Goma prison.

Adult and child prisoners being interviewed.

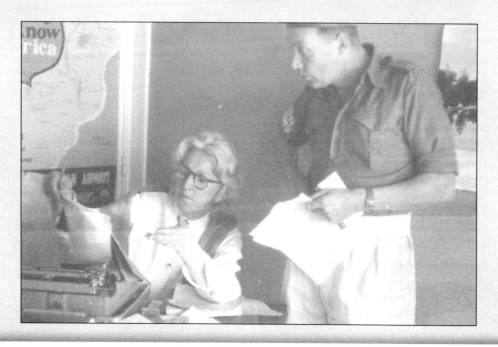

Capt. Reidy gets useful geographical information from former tour operator.

Sgt. M. Quinn, P. O'Connor,
C/S Kevin McCourt,
RSM Harrington.

On 'safari' patrol to Rwindi.

Comdt. Joseph Laffan and
CQMS. K. McCourt.

THE CONGO 1960 – The First Irish UN Peacekeepers

The back of a Land Rover is not a smooth ride.

Stopping for a break.

Hippos at a water hole.

African bull elephant.

Mrs. Six returns to her plantation to pay workers.

Coffee bean washing area.

Included in this picture are Swedish interpreter, Rev. Fr. C. Crean, Capt. Reidy, wife of the big game hunter who is on the extreme right, Comdt. Laffan and Spanish doctor.

Family members waiting to visit patients.

Typical countryside in the area.

Sunrise over Kivu.

Abandoned home typical of the type used by Europeans in the Congo.

I look around the hospital grounds.

have you tried the NEW tea?

PATTISON'S

LUXURY BLEND   "The Tea with a Tradition"

SUNDAY INDEPENDENT

VOL. 55. No. 31.   D   DUBLIN, SUNDAY, JULY 31, 1960.   PRICE FOURPENCE

All styles
POPLIN SHO
Prices
GALL
HENRY

DRAMATIC APPEAL FROM MR. HAMMARSKJOLD

UNO WANTS MORE IRISH TROOPS FOR THE CONGO

Taoiseach promises Government will decide within a week

UN. SECRETARY-GENERAL MR. DAG HAMMARSKJOLD HAS ASKED IRELAND TO SEND A SECOND BATTALION TO THE CONGO TO JOIN THE 32ND BATTALION FOR POLICE DUTY IN THE STRIFE-TORN REPUBLIC.

The Taoiseach, Mr. Lemass, who received the request, has replied

Wages

No mean task soldiers in the

COMMUNICATIONS WILL

Second Irish battalion for the Congo

A SECOND battalion of Irish troops will be airlifted to the Congo next week. The decision to send the new force, requested by the United Nations, was taken at a Government meeting to-day.

It is understood that the second force will be similar to the first with 650 men and officers.

Shortly after midday, the following statement was issued by the Government Information Bureau: "The Government have decided to comply with the request of the Secretary-General of U.N. that a second Irish Battalion should be sent to the Congo."

Army headquarters have been working full pace over the past few days on the assumption that the Government would decide in favour of sending the new battalion; and it expected that they will be in a position to announce the names of men chosen to-night.

In response to requests for volunteers over the past week, about 3,000 men put forward their names, and by the time the Government decision was announced, the Army had already drawn up a provisional list of officers and men.

Orders have been placed with Irish firms for rations for a minimum of ten days in case food supplies are not readily available in the Congo. On the previous occasion the rations were not required as the 32nd Battalion were able to secure food in the Kivu province.

The battalion will assemble at the Curragh for documentation, dental charting, inoculation and familiarisation with conditions and customs in the Congo.

[Evening Press, Tuesday, 9 August 1960]

Having breakfast at the Royal Hotel.

The band and their fans outside 'Sainte Maria' church.

Lt. Col. Buckley ponders a musical problem with members of the band

We are invited to the official residence of the Lord Mayor of Leopoldville.

The pipes and drums always attract a crowd.

Signalman Keys and myself, outside the city.

General Van Horn arrives for United Nations Day celebrations.

Signalman Keys and I swim and relax at the Funa Club.

Tribal dance display.

Louis Armstrong sings for the audience.

The great trumpeter performs.

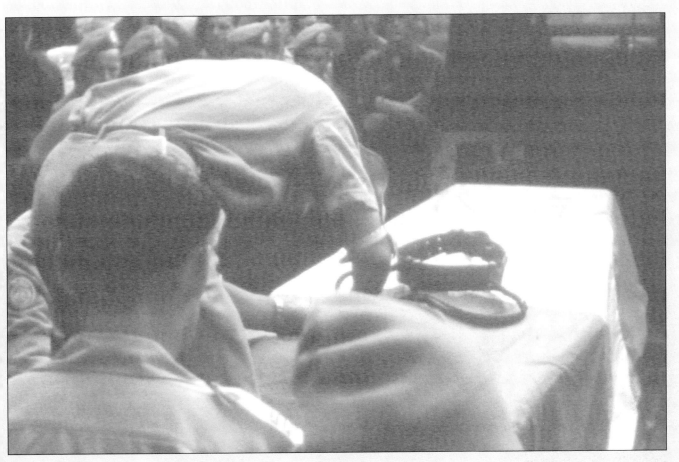

The remains of Col. J. McCarthy is draped in the Irish tricolour.

Multi-national guard of honour for Col. J. McCarthy.

Katangan forces in Elizabethville.

The patrol halts for refreshments.

Chapter 9

Katanga

On returning to Goma, it was business as usual. There was the ongoing bid by Congolese troops to exert their authority in certain areas, particularly at key locations such as the airport. These situations required delicate and sometimes lengthy negotiations between the Irish and Congolese officers.

Mr. Hammarskjold was successful in securing the peaceful entry of UN troops into Katanga, easing the fears of the Congolese authorities to the possibility of unwanted outside intervention. There remained considerable hostility to a UN presence in many parts of the Congo, but particularly so in Katanga. The UN entry was subject to a number of conditions. Among the stipulations were that the UN agreed not to take control from Katanga's police or military forces or to deploy troops from Communist dominated countries.

Both the 32nd and 33rd Battalions had platoons in a number of locations throughout the Kivu province and also in Katanga. In Katanga some of these operated out of the former Belgian military base at Kamina in the south west of the province, while it was mostly members of the 33rd who policed the northwest.

Brigade headquarters (SCOMEP) for both battalions was at Elizabethville in the south and close to what was at that time, the Rhodesian border. Detached to SCOMEP headquarters, I boarded a DC3 Dakota at 7am on 5 November at Goma and, via Kindu and Kabalo, I finally made it to Elizabethville, a distance of nine hundred and seventy miles, two days later.

Air of tension
On approach to the airstrip at Kabalo, the pilot had advised the passengers to stay alert because, on

Patrol to Kilubi. Note attempt at minor protection using corrugated metal sheets on the side of the pick-up truck.

105

THE CONGO 1960 – The First Irish UN Peacekeepers

previous occasions, shots had been fired at approaching aircraft from the cover of the jungle around the airfield. Following three hours of flying over mainly dense jungle, it was good to be touching down and I was looking forward to stretching my legs while the aircraft refuelled. There was an understandable air of tension on board as we scanned the surrounding bush for signs of movement or the reflection of the sun on a rifle barrel. In any event the Dakota smoothly descended making a perfect three-point landing without incident. While still rolling, as the DC3 reached the end of the runway, the pilot pushed forward on the starboard throttle. With a lively roar the great air-cooled radial engine swung the aircraft through one hundred and eighty degrees and, with the sound of both engines harmonised, she backtracked to the holding point.

As the door in the fuselage side was opened, the passengers were met by a surge of warm air. Outside were smiling faces of Ethiopian and Indian United Nations soldiers. Three of the welcoming party wore blue berets while the other two wore turbans and were bearded. The taller of the two turban wearers moved forward to meet the small group, who had jumped down from the doorway onto the hot tarmac. He explained that he and his small group had little or no

contact with their headquarters in this isolated area and that supplies of rice and other food items were either very low or had run out altogether. Their duties, and the conditions in which they carried them out, were similar to that which many small groups of men operated all over this vast and troubled country.

He told how they were based just a few miles from a very remote village and some weeks earlier had become aware of increasing activity and excitement there. As their mandate was to observe and try to maintain peace, they kept a close but discreet watch on developments, particularly if there were any signs of mercenary activities. None had occurred and relationships between themselves and the villagers remained good.

Horrific story

He went on to relate a horrific story. Tom-toms beat out a rhythm one afternoon in the village and the sound carried clearly through the jungle to the UN camp. With no apparent signs of anything untoward developing and no indications of a threat to their safety, the men remained calm but alert. Towards evening the entire population of the village seemed to be in celebratory mode as unified groups pounded the earth to the hypnotic rhythm of the drums and chanted harmoniously as they moved around the village's

Katangan armour. The U.N. had nothing like this at the time.

ceremonial enclosure. It was as if they were under the direction of a choreographer. After many hours of dancing and singing there was much feasting and the observers concluded that they had witnessed perhaps an annual ancient tribal event or ritual.

One of the tribe was well educated and acted as interpreter to the UN group who had gained his confidence. Some days had passed before he outlined the background and the detail of what had taken place in the village.

Missionaries had come to Africa for a hundred years and more and, although many stations had closed because of the recent violence, some chose to stay. One such missionary was a nun who had come to this remote part of the Congo as a young woman over forty years earlier. She had lived with, and loved, the local people and now, well on in years, the children she had nourished in mind and body were themselves adult senior members of the tribe. She had helped to bring the Christian message to the area in harmony with strong tribal customs and the influences of the much-respected Witch Doctor.

With anarchy and rebellion in the air the Witch Doctor decided it might be a good time to become the number one man for all healing in the village and put it to his people that should the ageing nun die naturally, or be killed by a rival tribe, all the good and obvious benefits which she was associated with in the village would either leave with her spirit or pass on to whoever would be responsible for her death. Using the words of Jesus, 'take and eat this is my body', he successfully convinced the people that the only way to ensure their continued good fortune and happiness would be the sacrifice of the nun.

Tales of slavery and cannibalism were recorded in the diaries of Dr. Charles Edward Roche Gardner, an Irish medical doctor who accompanied a group of fifteen Europeans to central Africa towards the end of the nineteenth century. The Belgian Government tried to stop the practice but it is said to have continued in some areas into the first half of the twentieth century. It seemed a little of it was still going on ...

Stranded at Kamina

With clouds closing in, the pilot was anxious to be away on the next leg of the journey. Although only a brief refuelling stop one hoped that the meeting with fellow UN personnel would be a morale booster for the men at Kabalo. At least their letters were now on the way to their families in distant lands.

Soon the DC3 was enveloped in turbulent cloud and buffeting its way through a storm. One of the great workhorses of the sky, flying extensively all over the world since 1935, this unique aircraft is an all-time favourite of aviation buffs today. The distinctive sound, smell and amazing STOL (short take off and landing) capabilities on unforgiving landing strips, are just some of the attributes, which makes her so special. The pilots who flew the DC3 were extraordinary in their own right and possessed an affinity with the aircraft. Without accurate weather reports they could set out from a remote airstrip, fly for hours over dense inhospitable jungle and land at what would sometimes be no more than a clearing in the bush. Without today's advanced navigational aids and meteorological forecasts the pilots somehow managed to find and land at their intended location.

Alas, when this particular flight finally reached Kamina, having endured severe buffeting, the aircraft became unserviceable and was grounded. I received information that a C119 was leaving for Elizabethville a short time later and was driven at high speed in an effort to be on the flight. On arrival at the airport the aircraft was already taxiing out for takeoff. Temporarily stranded at Kamina and not knowing when my journey would continue, I made arrangements to stay there until the next available flight.

On patrol

The next morning, Sunday, 6 November, I attended open air Mass at 6.30am, celebrated by Fr. Brophy. With no news of possible flights that day, I decided to accompany a patrol to Kilubi. This remote and isolated outpost was one of many guarded by UN troops throughout the Congo. Belgian officers led the Gendarmerie in Katanga and this irritated the Baluba population, who were in the majority. The Balubas were pro-Lumumba and wished to see the end of control by 'whites', Belgian or otherwise. They engaged the Katangan forces at Manono, Luena, Niemba, Kabalo and Mitwaba and, generally because of the superior firepower of their adversaries, they suffered heavy losses. In some instances, intervention by Irish UN forces helped to avert clashes between the rival factions. UN patrols, sent to investigate reports of trouble, sometimes arrived after a massacre had already occurred and the only thing they could then do was to count the dead and report on the incident from whatever intelligence could be gathered at the scene.

As our patrol pressed on towards Kilubi, we passed seven truckloads of Katangan troops heading in the same direction. When the outpost was reached, it was clear from the welcome extended to the patrol, that the guard being relieved were happy to be vacating the remote post. There was no delay in changing the guard and within thirty minutes of arriving, the return journey was under way.

The roads on the return journey had changed, literally, into riverbeds. It was now the rainy season and roads, which were not great when dry, could become mud tracks in a matter of minutes. There was an almost frightening intensity to the tropical storms. Holes and bumps in what used to be a road were rendered invisible by the downpour and it took great skill on the part of the drivers just to stay on track.

Although journey time was considerably increased, it was preferable to reach our destination at a slower pace rather than risk a breakdown in remote and possibly hostile territory. After eight hours of being tossed about in a Landrover, it was good to get back to base, have a meal and relax for a while.

I finally reached Elizabethville the next day, flying southwest from Kamina in a DeHavilland Beaver. After a briefing with Capt Bunworth at SCOMEP Headquarters, I booked into a room in the Hotel Katanga. Being in a city, I took the opportunity to replenish film stock, and I dispatched previously developed rolls of film to Capt. Jack Miller, back in Dublin.

On Wednesday, 9 November, I awoke to find my wristwatch had stopped. Not sure of the time, I immediately went to HQ to receive my orders and then, as it was only 8am, went out to have breakfast. I spent the day taking photographs around the city and while doing so observed Katangan troops checking civilians for passes. I noticed a Gendarmerie truck loaded with prisoners and was reminded of the unrest that prevailed in Katanga Province. On returning to HQ in the evening, news had just filtered through that an Irish patrol, attached to the 33rd Battalion, had been ambushed at Niemba and that some of them were feared dead.

The remote Kilubi outpost.

Chapter 10

First Casualties

The telex message received at SCOMEP Headquarters was without much detail and it would be some time before all the facts were known.

I was ordered to Niemba to record anything, which might be of value. With no immediate means of reaching Niemba quickly, I was forced to await the first available aircraft going in that direction. To go by road was considered suicidal without a strong escort and this option was immediately ruled out. Information from Elizabethville airport about aircraft movements usually reached our office too late to be

of any use. I made several dashes to the airport over the next few days, only to see the aircraft making its takeoff run or having just left minutes earlier. Eventually, at 7am on 14 November I was aboard a DC3, which had Albertville on its flight plan. Albertville was 390 miles away by air but the aircraft was scheduled to take a circular route, with my destination at the end of the flight. This added nearly an additional 1000 miles to the journey but I had learned by now it was a case of 'take it or leave it'. Not knowing when there might be another flight it was

Lt. Col. Bunworth O.C. 33rd. Battalion.

usually a 'take it' decision. The first leg of the journey was northwest to Kamina, with further landings at Kabalo and Kindu. At 600 miles, Kindu was about the halfway point and I was looking forward to the next stop, which was Goma and was familiar to me. Within half an hour of taking off from Kindu, the weather deteriorated and a raging storm buffeted the aircraft severely. There was no way through it and the pilot wisely returned to Kindu.

A Colonel's invitation

As I jumped down from the door of the DC3, a man dressed in boots, fatigue slacks and a string vest approached me. Pointing to my Air Corps collar badges he inquired what unit I was with. When he heard that I was a UN photographer from the Irish Air Corps, he introduced himself as an American Air Force Colonel and invited me to stay the night with his flight crew.

Instructing one of his men to look after me, he returned to whatever he was doing. As I walked away with my escort, I looked back to see him unloading stores from a Globemaster with some other airmen. "Is he really a Colonel?" I asked, and in a drawl tinged with admiration my question was answered, "you bet he is!". I had no reason to doubt my host's credentials but I had never seen a Colonel, stripped to the waist and perspiring as he toiled with his men. Before 1960 the Irish Defence Forces had little if any active contact with military personnel from other countries. A lot has been learned since those early days and now over forty years later the Irish Defence Forces are recognised leaders in the field of peacekeeping and peace enforcing.

The task of the American crew I had just acquainted was to fly Nigerian UN peacekeepers into Kindu to relieve the Mali troops who had been based here for a few months. The Americans had set up a compound measuring about 20 metres by 10 metres enclosed with two-metre high canvas walls or screens. A row of metal folding beds, with mattresses, was arranged along two opposite walls. The familiar jungle sounds of remote airfields such as this, was interrupted by the distinct noise of a small petrol driven generator motor. This was used to provide lighting and most importantly electricity to power a large fridge where perishable foods and a large supply of whiskey were kept.

Arrived in Goma

That night, the Mali troops were in celebratory mood as they looked forward to flying out. One played a harmonica and another a type of tin whistle and I was encouraged to join in with a few tunes on my trumpet. The party went on well into the night but I took to my allocated bed about midnight. No doubt the whiskey supplied by the Americans contributed to the sound

sleep I got that night. I really did sleep sound because it was not until next morning that I was aware of the mosquito bites all over my stomach. After a quick mug of coffee and a few biscuits I took leave of my American fellow airmen and was airborne by 7am.

A couple of hours later I landed at Goma. At first I was surprised to see Capt. Brady and Sergeant Rowe standing on the tarmac but then I remembered the typical dash to the airport on hearing the sound of an aircraft during the time that I was stationed there. They told me that the 32nd Battalion had been moved to Kamina and they were the only two Irish soldiers left in Goma. Although there was only an hour before taking off again, there was just enough time to have breakfast with them at a small hotel in the town.

The scenery was stunning as we flew south over Lake Kivu and Lake Tangyanika. With a good meal inside me, and my eyes feasting on the magnificent panorama of the African countryside, the two and a half-hour flight seemed remarkably short.

On reporting to 33rd Battalion Headquarters, the Sgt. Major arranged accommodation for me with the Military Police, who were occupying an abandoned bungalow.

Balubas on the warpath

A couple of months earlier, Lt Col. R.W.Bunworth had made the best use of the troops under his command to keep roads open and protect the many towns and villages spread widely throughout North Katanga. Removing roadblocks and repairing damaged bridges were regular features of most patrols. Baluba war parties were often encountered. There were instances when Balubas, under the influence of 'bangi-bangi', a local drug, would appear from the surrounding bush as a patrol cut its way through a road block or replaced planks on a bridge.

By early October, Niemba had been over-run by Baluba and, with the exception of a few buildings, had been burnt to the ground. They took many prisoners and killed anyone who would not co-operate by joining them. As the resolve by the Baluba to eliminate all European influence grew, so too the Gendarmerie reacted with equal resolve not to let it happen.

On 5 October, a patrol led by Comdt. Keogh entered Niemba and found it deserted. It transpired that a heavily armed Gendarmerie unit had paid a visit to the village on the previous night, and attacked and massacred a number of Balubas. The Gendarmerie claimed that they had only fired in self-defence.

To afford some protection to the local population, Col. Bunworth decided to establish an outpost in Niemba. A patrol was sent out and as a temporary measure, Sgt. J. Guthrie and a small party set up a base while the rest of the patrol returned to Albertville.

On the same day, Lt. Kevin Gleeson and half his platoon flew out of Kamina Base. They had been selected to garrison Niemba. They reached Albertville on 6 October and two days later took up their new posting in Niemba. Their spirits were high and they had been looking forward to a change of routine, not to mention scenery. They set about making their new home as comfortable as possible. When Sgt. Guthrie's group returned to Albertville a few days later they moved to the buildings, which had been previously occupied by the interim guard.

Patrols got under way immediately and roadblocks on the approaches to the village were manned. These activities gave reassurance to those locals who had fled into the bush to survive the earlier massacre and some began to return to the area. Lt. Gleeson's platoon took their work seriously, burying the dead and making friends with the locals. They employed a couple of locals for odd jobs around the camp. Offering medical help, a feature of many newly established Irish UN posts, although not officially part of their mission, was also helpful in gaining the trust of the natives. The medical orderly, Matty Farrell, did what he could with his limited supplies.

Slow progress

Outside the village, the dreaded roadblocks and hostile Baluba were a constant worry. Reinforcements under Comdt. P.D. Hogan arrived to lend support to Lt. Gleeson and his men, and help in their difficult task at Niemba. A patrol of forty men, in a variety of vehicles, travelled south from Niemba one day in early November, but made slow progress due to the number of roadblocks. The Baluba were gathered in great numbers and were intent on war. Another patrol under Comdt. Barry was heading north from Manono. By comparison they encountered friendly Baluba.

The intention was that both patrols were to keep going until they met each other. The task proved more difficult than expected and they each returned to their respective bases as time ran out, without meeting up. When Lt. Gleeson returned to Niemba he was delighted to find that the rest of his platoon had arrived from Albertville.

A couple of days later, on the 9 November, Lt. Gleeson decided to patrol the Manono road. The two vehicles used were a Volkswagen pick-up and a Landrover. They came across the usual obstacles and at the first trench put down planks and continued on their

WED 9th Nov. '60
This morning I awoke to find my watch stopped so I immediately went to H.Q. and gave Capt Bunworth some negatives to be delivered to Capt Miller. It was only eight o'clock so I went for a bit of breakfast. After that I. went for a long walk and took some shots around Eliz'th. After lunch Comdt Dayle asked me to inquire about exposure metres for him, which I did and gave him the information at 18.15 hrs. News came in about a patrol of nine Irish men being killed by Baluba tribesmen in Albertville.

Extract from the Author's Diary.

111

way. They crossed three more trenches before reaching the bridge over the river Luweyeye. It was not unusual as a patrol approached an obstacle, to see Baluba run for the cover of the bush. However it was noticed that on this occasion they appeared to be armed and this caused the men to become a little anxious.

The ambush
This was routine for some members of the patrol, but for those who had just rejoined their old section, it was a new experience. Lt. Gleeson, Sgt. Gaynor and Private Kenny surveyed the damaged bridge. They decided it might be possible to go around the bridge and cross the river at a shallow point. While Kenny set about clearing a path with a shovel, Gleeson, Gaynor, Dougan and Kelly crossed the river and walked down the road on the other side of the bridge to see if there were any more obstacles. What they saw was a large Baluba war party advancing on them.

It was crystal clear that negotiation was not going to stop this screaming crazed band of warriors. Lt.Gleeson called out "jambo" but the Balubas' only response was to fire a hail of arrows. We were all very much aware of the UN directive not to open fire unless fired upon. With the war party practically on top of them, and having been hit already with an arrow, Lt. Gleeson finally gave the order to fire. At least fifteen Baluba were killed and perhaps twelve wounded during this first return of fire.

With Baluba now coming at them from two directions, Lt. Gleeson called to his men to take cover. The attack happened so suddenly that it was not possible to reach the vehicles and so the two Bren guns, which they had brought with them, were not used. They ran down a small path that led to the river and made for high ground on the other side. The situation seemed well out of hand at this stage and arrows had hit several of the peacekeepers. The men must have been aware, that with their limited firepower up against such overwhelming odds, it was only a matter of time before they all died.

Lt. Gleeson's men joined him in prayer as more than a hundred Baluba pressed home their attack. These warriors, having undergone a form of baptism, believed bullets could not touch them. Believing in this protection and in a crazed state, they charged. Gleeson, Dougan, Kelly and McGuinn all died where they made their last stand.

Just before he was cut down, Lt. Gleeson called to his men to run for their lives. As they tried to get away from their attackers, a second arrow hit Kenny. The remaining six tried to put some distance between themselves and their now unstoppable killers. The high grass prevented the Irish from seeing each other and staying together to repel their attackers. Through

loss of blood and exaustion, Kenny fell as he tried to make his way through a swampy area. They again made an effort to get further away but Kenny fell a second time. He was joined by Anthony Brown and they stayed low as they listened to their attackers hacking their way towards them.

Lying face down in the mud, Kenny could hear the Balubas getting ever closer. When they were but a few paces away, he was aware of them pausing and then a third arrow pierced his neck. Perhaps they were running short of arrows, for they pulled this one out again. Bearing the pain, he lay still, hoping they would leave him for dead, but it was not to be. They beat him with clubs, first to the head and then all over his body. The pain was unbearable and he wished he were dead but also prayed that the beating would stop. This prayer was answered. Another burst of machinegun fire drew the Baluba off Kenny. They left him and chased after Brown who was firing his Gustaf. Speaking to Kenny a few weeks later at the hospital in Elizabethville, he related to me the horrific tale.

Grim discovery
When Lt. Gleeson's patrol did not return to base that evening, Cpt. Lynch became worried and contacted headquarters. As the evening wore on and with no sign still of the patrol, it was decided by Col. Bunworth to send a section under Lt. J. Enright to investigate.

At Niemba the situation was tense. The usual African night sounds, which everyone had come to be familiar with, were missing and as a precaution, hand grenades were primed. This was a common occurrence and I recall assisting an infantryman prime a box of grenades during a potentially serious situation at Goma airport a couple of months previously. It was hardly in the job description of an airman, but in the Congo nothing was normal. I looked on it as on-the-job training.

Once again, because of the time of year, the roads were veritable mud tracks and Lt. Enright's patrol arrived two hours later than their estimated time of arrival. To Capt. Lynch's relief, they finally reached Niemba at 3.45am. Pausing only to have a quick snack, Lt. Enright set out for the bridge an hour later with twenty-seven men and they reached their destination as dawn was breaking. It was not long before empty magazines and cartridges – the signs of battle – were discovered. A further search revealed four bodies. These were Lt. Kevin Gleeson, Sgt. Hugh Gaynor, Pte Michael McGuinn and Pte. Liam Dougan.

During the previous night, Fitzpatrick had stayed in hiding and as the morning drew nearer, he decided to move closer to the road. Fortunately for him, it was the correct move and it put him within earshot of Lt. Enright's patrol. Treated for shock, but otherwise uninjured, he was now safe. There was a lot of movement in the bush and it became obvious that this was still a very dangerous place to be. The situation was radioed to headquarters and the patrol was ordered back to Niemba.

The next day a patrol left Albertville under Comdt. P. D. Hogan, while from the south, Comdt. Barry led a patrol out of Manono. They encountered a very large party of Baluba travelling in trucks and, when questioned, they claimed to be reinforcements for the Baluba at Niemba. Col. Bunworth decided the risk was too great to proceed and ordered Comdt. Hogan back to Manono to assemble a stronger force, which would set out next morning.

Comdt. Barry's patrol, approaching from the south, arrived at a bridge over the Lukuga River and discovered that it had been badly damaged. The planks, which had been thrown into the river, were retrieved and the bridge repaired by engineering officer, Lt.Raftery, and his men. The search party was further strengthened by Ethiopian UN troops. That day they uncovered the body of Cpl. Peter Kelly. As the light was fading, the patrol returned to Niemba with the five bodies so far recovered from Lt. Gleeson's patrol.

On Thursday, November 10th, Comdt. Hogan's now strengthened search party made an early start and just after 7am they noticed a figure in UN uniform. It was Kenny.

The patrol was delighted to find another survivor and a rousing cheer went up. Congratulated on his escape by Capt. Crowley and Comdt. Hogan, Kenny, when asked who he was, simply replied "57 Kenny, Sir, reporting". These words have found a lasting place in the annals of Irish Military History. Kenny's will and determination to survive had sustained him through two nights of intense pain and he was at times delirious. At other times he was able to evaluate his situation and fortunately for him made reasoned decisions to avoid capture. Having received medical attention, he was airlifted by helicopter, accompanied by Dr. Heaney, back to Niemba.

Soon the bodies of Killeen, Farrell and Fennell were found and the search continued for Trooper Anthony Brown, alas without immediate success.

Delayed

Due to the acute shortage of aircraft and the all too common cancellations of flights, it was five days before I was aboard another DC3 in an attempt to reach Niemba. The plan was to fly one thousand miles north via Kindu to Goma, and then three hundred and twenty miles south to Albertville. However one hundred miles out from Kindu, once again, a severe storm necessitated a return to Kindu for the night. The journey was eventually completed the following day.

On night patrol with the Military Police of the 33rd Battalion, the town of Albertville was noticeably quiet and in the aftermath of the Baluba ambush there was a distinct feeling of tension in the air.

As we proceeded through the town, *en route* to the airport to attend a service for the victims of Niemba, the pavements were lined with Congolese civilians. They stood in silence as an expression of sorrow, and of their opposition to the Baluba actions. Moise Tshombe, the president of Katanga, whose assembly had declared the province independent, arrived at the airport at 11am and immediately walked to the hangar mortuary. A United Nations flag covered each of the coffins of Lt. Kevin Gleeson, Sgt. Hugh Gaynor, Liam Dougan, Michael McGuinn, Peter Kelly, Matty Farrell, Gerry Killeen, Thomas Fennell and William Davis. Tshombe stood in silence, head bowed, before the line of peacemakers who had given their lives as part of the ongoing effort to bring peace and stability to his country. After laying a floral wreath, he then turned to Lt. Col. Bunworth and spoke to him for some minutes.

At least ten armed jeeps escorted Tshombe away, and he returned two days later for a Mass service, celebrated by the Rev. Fr. Crowley. The enormous numbers of United Nations personnel from many nations as well as Congolese Government officials and civilians was a clear indication of the feeling of grief felt by all. The bodies were airlifted back to their homeland, plunged into grief by the devastating news of the massacre.

On 22 November there was a national day of mourning with masses being offered and special prayers said for the heroes of Niemba. People in Dublin wept openly as they witnessed Ireland's greatest-ever military funeral tribute.

It was apparent that because of the small numbers of UN personnel available to police an area so vast, it might be wiser to withdraw. The huge numbers of Lulua and Baluba warriors, stretched for hundreds of miles along the Congo basin, would be uncontrollable should the unrest continue. Against such overwhelming odds no small group could hope to keep order, if attacked, even armed with modern artillery. Bad roads, together with thick scrub, as described earlier, grass as tall as a man, hills, ravines and jungle, made the area ideal to launch a sudden ambush.

The depth of hatred by the Baluba in the area for all white people had now been brutally demonstrated. It would require a much greater UN force than was available to control the area. Having assessed the strategic importance or otherwise of the area, and with the peacekeepers spread thinly throughout vast areas of the Congo, it was decided to evacuate from Niemba.

Patrols still went out and continued the work of maintaining peace in so far as they could. Routine

113

patrols, as well as the search parties for Anthony Browne, were strengthened. The body of Trooper Brown was not found until exactly two years later when a combined Irish and Malayan search party discovered the remains. That mission was a dangerous one, as the Congolese army was by now in control of the area and was sympathetic to the Baluba. In the intervening time not a lot had changed in North Katanga and local chiefs and elders continued to influence their tribesmen.

Villages burning

Flying up to Niemba in a Sikorski-S55 helicopter, I could see many villages in blazing ruins. This was either the result of actions between Katanga troops and Baluba, or the tactic of Baluba in exacting scorched earth tactics on those who would not join them. Or possibly, it could have been the outcome of inter-tribal warfare. Whatever occurred, the scenes below brought home the extent of bloodletting that was happening. Numerous roadblocks were in evidence. As figures came into view down below, they would quickly vanish into the undergrowth or jungle at the sound of the approaching helicopter.

At one point we came across an encounter, which warranted a closer look. A number of apparently lifeless bodies, most likely Baluba, lay on the ground as a small patrol of Katangan soldiers stood by their jeeps waving to us with their bush hats.

On reaching Niemba, I slid the main door of the helicopter to the fully open position to provide a clear unobstructed view of the ambush location. Having filmed and photographed the area it became apparent how it was possible to be ambushed at this location. By the time we returned to base we had been two and a half hours in the air and I had a considerable amount of movie and still film, which I immediately parcelled for dispatch to my boss, Capt. Jack Miller back at Military Headquarters in Dublin.

As reports of numerous killings came in during the following days, there was concern for the safety of some nuns, who had chosen to stay on at their convent nearby. There was a small grassy area adjacent their chapel, which was used as a landing pad for the helicopters. It was only large enough for one helicopter to set down, so the two choppers took it in turn to land and evacuate the nuns.

Hospitalised

On 23 November, I was once again aboard the old reliable DC3 flying back to SCOMEP Headquarters in Elizabethville. The reason for the transfer was that Colonel Byrne, Chief of Staff in Ireland was about to visit the Congo. I was to accompany him on his tour of Irish bases. A couple of days later, at 8am, I was aboard a single engine de Havilland Beaver with the Chief to begin his tour. An hour and ten minutes into the flight, the familiar unpredictable weather changed. Thunder clouds boomed above the noise of the engine and lightning flashes lit up the darkened sky. The aircraft was like a small boat being tossed about in a heavy sea. The pilot decided to abort the flight. Helped by a strong tail wind we were back safely on the runway at Elizabethville in 45 minutes.

On 1 December I became feverish and had my temperature taken by an Italian medical orderly. It was a strange experience from feeling well to suddenly becoming alternatively very cold and then extremely hot. I was admitted to hospital, where the UN staff told me I was their first military patient. Within 24 hours the situation changed and I was no longer on my own. Privates Kenny and Fitzpatrick, the two Niemba survivors, and a few others were admitted before being flown back to Ireland. I was glad of the company and that night Joseph Kenny related his horrifying experience to me. When I awoke on Sunday 4th, my fellow patients had left the hospital.

Within three days I felt well enough to return to work but the doctor refused to give me the 'all clear'. Although I was officially on the hospital books for a further week, I was able to dine out and walk about Elizabethville for a bit of exercise. In the evening I met up with Company Quarter Master Sgt. Peelo, Sgt. Egan and Corporal Anderson who were on the very small numbers of Irish attached to the staff at SCOMEP Headquarters.

Europeans were understandably nervous of travelling without an escort in the Congo. The daughter of one UN advisor had been staying with friends in Northern Rhodesia, and he and his wife were naturally concerned for her. Wanting to have her close to the family, particularly as the troubles were escalating, I volunteered to go to Kitwe in Rhodesia and escort her back to Elizabethville.

Once over the border, the comparison with life in the Congo was striking. Passing through the town of Bancroft, it was business as usual and it was good to see shops, cinemas and other services operating normally, a far cry from where I had come from just a few hours previously. The two-day round trip by road was a small diversion from the usual routine and was completed successfully and without incident.

IRISHMEN SLAUGHTERED IN CONGO AMBUSH

Ten soldiers feared dead

TEN Irish soldiers of the United Nations Congo Force are feared to have been killed by Baluba tribesmen in an ambush in Katanga while on patrol. Conflicting agency reports and bad local communications make it difficult to be sure of the precise number of men killed.

However, as we go to press, seven bodies of the eleven-man patrol have been found, and one man is in hospital gravely ill. The uniforms of the remaining men have been found at the site of the ambush. This, together with the fact that the Baluba are known never to take prisoners, only leaves a slim hope for the safety of these men.

The ambush took place last night at Niemba, about 60 miles west of Albertville, while the patrol was engaged in removing a road block on the route to Manono. While no names of the dead men will be issued until next-of-kin have been informed, it is believed that the troops belonged to A Company of the 33rd Battalion.

[Evening Press, Wednesday, 9 November 1960]

Mr. Tshombe at the memorial service for the Niemba ambush victims.

Lt Col. Bunworth and Mr. Tshombe in conversation.

Final tributes on African soil.

My transport to Niemba.

Abandoned village near Niemba.

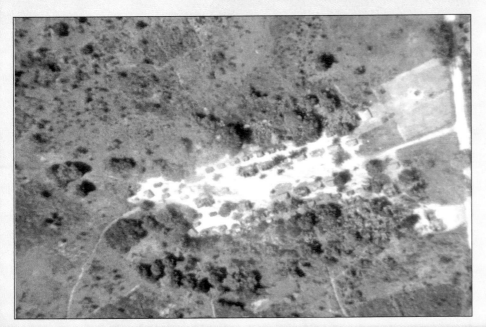

One of many burning villages on the way to Niemba.

Sunday Review

NOVEMBER 20, 1960 Vol. 4 No. 157 4d.

31 Westmoreland St., Dublin, Phone 75871

THE GRIEF AND THE GLORY...

AN IRISH SOLDIER COMES HOME

The roadblock at Niemba where the terrible ambush took place.

Niemba survivor, Pte. Joseph Kenny (right) following medical treatment and rest in Elizabethville pictured here with a Swedish UN soldier.

119

Niemba heroes are flown home to Ireland.

Final journey out of Africa begins.

Typical terrain en route to Niemba.

Chapter 11

Homeward Bound

By way of contrast to the conditions and duties of the majority of those who served during the first six months of Congo service, a very small number had a relatively comfortable time. Administration was obviously vital to the success of the entire operation also and the small numbers of Irish personnel stationed at Leopoldville and Elizabethville headquarters worked long hours to ensure that anything that could be done to assist their comrades in the field, was done. The advantages were that they worked in neat offices, lived in comfortable quarters and dined in quality restaurants and hotels. They also got the opportunity to visit the private homes of some Europeans who had stayed in the Congo and were now assisting the UN.

Compared to the virtual ghost towns near a lot of other postings, the shops in the cities, as well as the regular markets, were by and large operating normally and were reasonably well stocked. In even the remotest areas it was generally possible to buy small hand crafted souvenirs from individual local craftsmen. The men became adept at haggling with the traders, only paying a fraction of the initial asking price. The only limitations were the amount of money one had, or the weight of personal baggage each soldier was allowed to take back to Ireland.

I returned to Albertville, where the 33rd Battalion were stationed, on 23 December and on Christmas Eve set up a dark room in order to continue processing film.

Clear skies

Christmas day in Albertville had clear skies and was warm and sunny. Another first time experience for the Irish overseas. Except for the climate and special dinners held in the dining halls of the officers, sergeants, corporals and men, it was a day like any other. Naturally everyone thought of family back home, but right then family was the Battalion.

Visiting the separate dining halls of the men, corporals and sergeants, I filmed and took photographs as they enjoyed their Christmas dinner. When all had eaten, Sgt. Major D. Douglas and myself sat down to our meal. With my trusty trumpet, I contributed to the merriment in the NCOs' Mess on Christmas night.

Outposts, like the one at Bendera, had to be kept supplied with the necessities of life. As well as the obvious requirement to satisfy the physical needs of the troops in outlying areas, their psychological needs were equally important. The receipt of letters from home, and contact with their comrades in arms as they delivered the mail from platoon headquarters, helped in combating the feeling of isolation.

The patrols were, in comparison with those of a couple of months earlier, much larger and on this one to Bendera I counted nine vehicles. At Bendera, the night patrol encountered Baluba activity three miles out from the camp and returned for reinforcements. No one was ever off-duty in a situation such as this and everyone was a part of the follow-up operation. In this instance no contact was made and the platoon returned to camp as dawn was breaking.

Relief troops delayed

On the last day of 1960, Brigadier Ward and Major Francis Fanvyi of the Nigerian Army arrived at Albertville. Nigerian troops were to relieve the 33rd Battalion, whose tour of duty was to end in a couple of week's time. The Brigadier was on a tour of inspection to familiarise himself with the area and check out the facilities available before taking over. As the tour of inspection continued, the Irish Signals Corps picked up information that the relief Battalion was having some difficulties in reaching Albertville. The train they were travelling on had come under attack about twelve miles out. Concerned for his troops, the Brigadier decided to investigate the situation immediately. There was a quick pre-flight briefing with the Sikorski pilot who had flown him in a few hours earlier and he then set out to locate the train.

The only thing clear from the air was that the train was not going anywhere and judging by the mixture of Nigerian, Congolese troops and Baluba which could be identified, the situation was not going to improve without intervention. It was decided to land in a clearing close to the railway line. The Brigadier succeeded in resolving the situation and the train was permitted to proceed. All through the twenty minute 'parley' the helicopter rotors were kept turning in readiness for immediate takeoff, if the situation required it.

Another not dissimilar action took place three miles north of Mukulakulu where Swedish UN troops came under attack from hundreds of Baluba. They had come through several days of sporadic attack. In three concentrated attacks, the Baluba were finally repulsed sustaining heavy casualties.

It had become a regular occurrence for Baluba to remove sections of rail track in an attempt to prevent the movement of UN troops. Locomotives were also being burned at railway stations during the night. With only three days left before returning home these actions played heavily on the minds of the men at Albertville. There was a lot of conjecture or in soldiers' terms 'ball hops' going about as to how the 33rd Battalion would leave the base. It was no help when word came through that the relief train of Nigerians, mentioned earlier, was now stranded. The tracks had been torn up at both ends of the train.

Mission ends

Perhaps the Battalion could travel by boat to Usumbura and be flown out from there, but were there sufficient boats to move a Battalion? Maybe the move could be made by road. Even if sufficient transport could be acquired, bearing in mind the present state of unrest, this option was fraught with danger. These were anxious times as crates were packed and unnecessary kit burned in preparation for the big move out.

It was a great relief to all concerned when it was learned that DC4 aircraft could be used to airlift the Battalion to Kamina. On 10 January, the 33rd Battalion came together with the 32nd at Kamina, to where they had been moved some months previously, and both groups made final preparations for the journey home.

Two days later the first of the 34th Battalion were flown to the Congo to begin their six month long tour of duty. They fired questions at members of the two battalions, who had preceded them, as they were now veterans of the operation. No doubt, as they listened to the 'old sweats', the newcomers assumed some of the stories being related had embellishments added. They would, however, later realise from their own experiences that this was not the case.

Proven to be of great benefit in the past, the 34th Battalion also brought a pipe band with them. Founded only six months previously, I was pleased to see them as they were all former colleagues of mine, serving with the Air Corps at Baldonnel.

Friday 13th January, unlucky for some but lucky for us, was the day the journey home began. The discomforts of the long exhausting flight via Leopoldville, Kano and Wheelus were overwhelmed by the joy of returning, after a long absence, to our families in Ireland. The Globemaster finally settled onto the runway at Dublin Airport just after two o'clock on the morning of Monday 16 January 1961.

Thus ended what is now seen as the first chapter of service by an Irish battalion of United Nations troops. By the time the Congo operations came to an end in 1964, twenty-seven Irish soldiers had paid the ultimate price and given their lives in the service of peace.

Sun. 15th Jan. '61

Our aircraft touched down in Wheelus air base at 04.00 hrs. We had a good breakfast and were then billetted. After Mass I had a bit of a nap. After dinner I went with three of the lads to the American airforce N.C.O's club for a drink. We left Wheelus at 19.49 hrs and after a long and uncomfortable flight (my elbow was paining quite a bit) we landed in dear old Ireland at Collinstown

Extract from the Author's Diary.

Brigadier Ward receives informa-tion that his troops (coming to relieve us) are under siege.

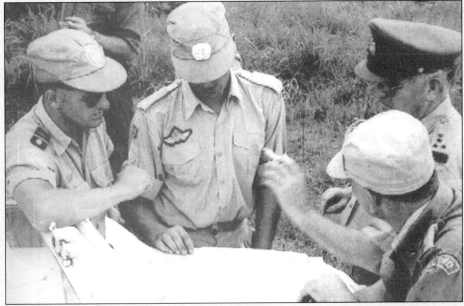

The Brigadier and Col. Bunworth establish the location of the train.

The Brigadier is allowed leave the helicopter, but a close eye is kept on me.

33rd. Battalion Military Police about to begin their night patrol in Albertville.

The 34th Battalion bring old Irish armoured cars with them.

The halted train of Nigerian U.N. troops is located.

Vital installations, such as this power station, are visited prior to hand over by the Irish.

A rail car at the Hydro power station, which takes workers and members of a local tribe to the top of the mountain.

We begin to board the Globemaster 'Dublin Express'.

African lightening is terrifying.

I pose with Jacko (Jacko in the middle) and Michael Kavanagh in Kamina.

The first of the 34th. Battalion and my colleagues from the Air Corps Pipe Band arrive in the Congo to begin their 6 months tour of duty.

Men of the 34th. move off to set up home in Africa.

33rd Battalion N.C.O.s on Christmas Day 1960.

Lt. Col. Bunworth with some of his men of the 33rd Battalion on Christmas Day.

Evening Mail

Dublin, Tuesday, January 17, 1961.   2d.

Making their happy return

L. to r.: Captain Donal Sweeney, Commandant Thomas Treacy, O.C., "A" Co., 32nd Batt. (first man to land at the airport on the Battalion's return), and Captain Noël Cantrell. They arrived home from the Congo this morning.

Personnel who served with the
32nd Infantry Battalion

(Rank at time of serving)

Very Rev. C.P. Crean
0.6014 Comdt. F. Fleming
0.5171 Comdt. P.F. Groghan
0.7434 Capt. J. Burke
0.6196 Capt. J. Duggan
0.7420 Capt. N.G. Cantrell
0.6208 Comdt. P.J. Liddy
0.7480 Capt. M.J. Duggan
0.7463 Capt. B.A. Deegan
0.7582 Lt.D.G. Houston
0.7829 Capt. E.D. Daly
0.7664 Lt. M.O.H. Wright
0.6386 Capt. P. Allen
0.7502 Lt. A.A. Riordan
0.7207 Capt. J. O'Dwyer

Rev. Fr. G. Brophy
0.5752 Comdt. J. Adams
0.7489 Capt. J. Fives
0.4955 Comdt. M.D. Hassey
0.4976 Comdt. W. O'Carroll
0.7547 Lt. H.E. Daly
0.4989 Comdt. T. Ryan
0.7536 Capt. D.K. Boyle
0.7718 Lt. J. Flynn
0.5030 Comdt.J.P. Laffan
0.6375 Comdt. T. Tracey
0.7522 Lt. C.D. O'Leary
0.7643 Lt. T.G. Harrington
0.5134 Comdt. P.J. Carroll
0.7482 Capt.J. Kissane

0.4909 Lt/Col. M.J. Buckley
0.4975 Comdt. M.J. O'Brien
0.6931 Capt. J. Moran
0.6893 Capt. J.C. Slye
0.5947 Capt. A.O. Cunningham
0.6370 Capt P. Reidy
0.6387 Capt. D. O'Suibhne
0.7811 Lt. E.T. Cassidy
0.6284 Capt. J.V.F. Brady
0.6745 Comdt. H.P.J. O'Shea
0.6628 Capt. A.R. Maynard
0.6377 Capt. E. Russell
0.7568 Lt. C.J. Fitzgerald
0.7162 Capt. D.A. Black
0.7503 Lt. F. Stewart

Military College
70901 BSM. P. O'Connor

803742 Pte. W. Morris

4 Inf. Bn.
79505 CQMS. H. Doyle
81911 Sgt. N. O'Brien
807740 Cpl. J. Lillis
92314 Cpl. R. Seaward
99626 Cpl. E. Shaw
94764 Cpl. D. Goggins
807200 Cpl. H. Cassidy
807201 Pte. T. Hayes
809198 Pte. P. Lynch
808289 Pte. P. O'Donavan
808893 Pte. C. Nugent
808962 Pte. P. O'Meara
809394 Pte. W. Fitzgerald
809158 Pte. C. Kelleher
808986 Pte. D. Mc.Carthy
803967 Pte. P. Grace
806697 Pte. T. Meagher
806555 Pte. P. O'Sullivan
808687 Pte. D. Corbett
804128 Pte. J. Murphy
808061 Pte. T. Buckley
809086 Pte. M. O'Shea
807759 Pte. J. Connolly
809535 Pte. D. Foley
808671 Pte. R. Raymond

430337 CS. W. Dullard
94557 Sgt. W. O'Sullivan
807690 Cpl. J. Murphy
806303 Cpl. M. Geary
802841 Cpl. G. Kent
809355 Cpl. M. Parker

802479 Pte. J. Woods
807199 Pte. P. Dennehy
805651 Pte. M. Wallace
809260 Pte. J. Spillane
808983 Pte. T. Lowe
809657 Pte. D. Fenton
809141 Pte. C. Gleeson
804374 Pte. D. O'Brien
809137 Pte. P. Flynn
808332 Pte. P. O'Regan
801389 Pte. F. Hayes
96796 Pte. D. Leahy
810384 Pte. J. Roche
806750 Pte. B. Roche
803627 Pte. J. Hogan
807232 Pte. J.C. Conway
808009 Pte. J. Lynch
807986 Pte. J. O'Connor

82108 Sgt. D. Condon
95023 Sgt. R. Irwin
807688 Cpl. D. Leahy
802646 Cpl. M. Higgins
807250 Cpl. E. Sharpe
804780 Cpl. B. Timoney

809379 Pte. M. Kelly
809210 Pte. P. O'Neill
809157 Pte. K. O'Riordan
806687 Pte. M. Keohan
94780 Pte. P. Roche
805482 Pte. J. Geary
806772 Pte. T. O'Brien
809258 Pte. T. Slattery
806862 Pte. J. Murphy
808161 Pte. D. Goulding
808432 Pte. J. Collins
808946 Pte. M. Mc.Loughlin
97480 Pte. C. O'Connor.
805059 Pte. T. O'Rahilly
805879 Pte. C. Twomey
809707 Pte. D. Crowley
809035 Pte. T. Sweeney
807233 Pte. D. O'Sullivan

1st Field Company Signals
95548 Cpl. B. Roche
808202 Pte. P. Ryan
807961 Pte. S. Kavanagh
807960 Pte. D. Tierney

809211 Cpl. J. King
808638 Pte.P. Hogan
808914 Pte. T. Barry
807958 Pte. P. Cullen

808961 Pte. W. O'Brien
808938 Pte. P. Dillon
807790 Pte.T. Sullivan

1st Field Company S&T
807345 Pte. J. Kelly

99139 Pte. R. O'Neill

1st Field Company COE

806463 Cpl. J. Kavanagh	808636 Pte. W. Gallanan	804726 Pte. J. Murphy
808639 Pte.E. O'Donnell	804745 Pte. P. Relihan	805717 Pte. T. Heffernan

1st FA Regiment

81359 Cpl. T. Walsh	91282 Cpl. J. Deegan	809496 Pte. T. Wade
809421 Pte.P. Murphy	809497 Pte. E. Mc.Grath	806874 Pte. C. Costelloe
809640 Pte. E. Carey	809472 Pte. W. Casey	806458 Pte. P. Donnelly
809432 Pte. J. Hayes	809473 Pte. J. Keane	809508 Pte. P. O'Gorman
809390 Pte. M. Young	809990 Pte. J. Barrett	809689 Pte. J. Cashin
808701 Pte. R. Donnelly		

1st Motor Squadron

91953 Cpl. W. Mulcahy	801014 Pte. J. Nolan	802907 Pte. D. Barry
82357 Pte. T. Mockler	808147 Pte. J. Curry	804017 Pte. D. Lehane
807825 Pte. J. Carey	808149 Pte. D. Roche	805124 Pte. W. Nolan
808134 Pte. P. O'Regan	804027 Pte. D. McManus	809311 Pte. P. Power

CT Depot South Comd.
802515 Cpl. W. Sisk

802123 Pte. J. Minihan

Comd. HQRS. South Comd.
808706 Cpl. J. Phelan

803693 Pte. S. Elsted

804676 Pte. P. Ryan

3rd G/Coy. AOC

808250 Cpl. D. Cusack	807890 Cpl. P. McCormack	801225 Pte. C. Harte
96387 Pte. T. Penkert		

3rd G/Coy. S&T
805435 Pte. J. Butler

3rd G/Coy. MPC
96435 Cpl. E. Heaphy

805021 Cpl. M. Murphy

3rd H/Coy. AMC

82133 Cpl. P. O'Donoghue	809363 Pte. T. Harmon	807177 Pte. M. Hoey
806128 Pte. M. Shiels		

3rd FA Regt.
806619 Cpl. T. O'Flaherty

802344 Pte. B. Brennan

3rd Brigade Hqrs.
87508 Sgt. D. Mahon

97238 Pte. M. Dundon

12th Infantry Battalion

87286 Sgt. W. Kane	88186 Cpl. A. Kelly	90301 Cpl. P. O'Donnell
98320 Cpl. J. Power	808906 Cpl. J. Mullins	94290 Cpl. E. Mc.Coy
803707 Pte. S. Walsh	807816 Pte. D. Culhane	808285 Pte. G. Hynes
806281 Pte. P. White	808637 Pte. P. Flynn	800636 Pte. P. Mullins
807239 Pte. J. O'Grady	808658 Pte. E. O'Reilly	809384 Pte. J. Foran
809240 Pte. J. Grimes	98543 Pte. W. Hoare	806943 Pte. J. Maloney
807254 Pte. E. Murphy	808816 Pte. M. Behan	99239 Pte. W. Walsh
805151 Pte. E. Fitzgerald	806961 Pte. W. Thornton	804904 Pte. A. Hussey
808703 Pte. L. Higgins	809006 Pte. J. Finnan	806978 Pte. P. Farrell
809171 Pte. M. O'Brien	807030 Pte. D. Casey	808642 Pte. C. Ryan
807520 Pte. J. Holden	810536 Pte. J. Barry	807956 Pte. P. Daly

808558 Pte. L. O'Meara
808959 Pte. D. Pollard
806796 Pte. M. Lysaght

808872 Pte. J. Laste
99573 Pte. J. Flynn

801016 Pte. S. Corbett
803765 Pte. N. Kelly

14th Inf. Bn.
804610 Cpl. S. O'Donoghue

806369 Pte. P. Troy

1st Inf. Bn.
801545 Sgt. W. Hegarty
95866 Pte. P. Corcoran
808614 Pte. M. O'Halloran
806517 Pte. P. Sharry
806635 Pte. M. Noone
806464 Pte. P. Quinn
805603 Pte. B. McDonagh
807996 Pte. M. King

805888 Cpl. M. McGowan
807710 Pte. P. Cooley
809637 Pte. M. Purcell
809956 Pte. G. Poole
809672 Pte. P. Walsh
809030 Pte. C. O'Donnell
810041 Pte. M. Laydon
809441 Pte. S. Murphy

810337 Pte. J. Dunne
806311 Pte. P. Flaherty
805680 Pte. J. Glynn
809275 Pte. P. Mannion
808211 Pte. M. Connole
70286 Pte. M. Flaherty
90307 Pte. T. Crowley
808615 Pte. P. Joyce

6th Inf. Bn.
87704 Sgt. R. McGrath
425332 Cpl. M. Lynch
806823 Cpl. D. Mullins
807328 Cpl. G. Malone
807712 Pte. P. Flynn
808048 Pte. P. Dixon
808956 Pte. J. Parkes
808118 Pte. F. Doherty
806438 Pte. T. Courtney
807711 Pte. M. Flynn
807029 Pte. T. Revins
809947 Pte. R. Bradley
807302 Pte. P. Bracken
809179 Pte. K. O'Sullivan
808266 Pte. M. Beirne
802356 Pte. M. Devanney

86481 Cpl. J. Keneghan
77836 Cpl. J. O'Brien
92657 Cpl. E. Dowling
94318 Cpl. R. Mc.Manus
809014 Pte. M. Tighe
808554 Pte. F. Boland
804875 Pte. P. Malone
808114 Pte. E. Gormley
808957 Pte. P. O'Neill
806721 Pte. J. Daly
92660 Pte. O'Hanlon
809854 Pte. D. Molloy
809693 Pte. N. Stanley
09084 Pte. J. Feery
801956 Pte. B. Conlon
810214 Pte. J. Nicell

803636 Cpl. J. Ryan
804862 Cpl. M. Dowler
807301 Cpl. P. McNally
808264 Cpl. P. Fogarty
809849 Pte. D. Manley
809130 Pte. J. Ganley
803890 Pte. P. O'Brien
806704 Pte. M. O'Sullivan
808977 Pte. J. Bracken
807357 Pte. J. Kelly
809174 Pte. J. Shanagher
809683 Pte. M. Brennan
809016 Pte. R. Larkin
05835 Pte. J. Silke
807891 Pte. P. Hall
809777 Pte. J. Redmond

16th Inf. Bn.
431370 CQMS. P. Whitney
90401 Pte. P. Moore

804551 Cpl. J. Bracken

805144 Pte. T. Maloney

17th Inf. Bn.
75543 Sgt. J. Manning

805374 Cpl. J. Conlon

18th Inf. Bn.
806980 Cpl. G. Tierney

806506 Cpl. J. Kenny

19th Inf. Bn.
807243 Cpl. M. Byrne

803227 Cpl. P. Dennedy

803925 Pte. M. Lannon

4th F/Coy. COE.
78049 C/S C. Byrne
808607 Pte. J. Devlin
806411 Pte. J. Cox
94301 Pte. D. Connolly
807703 Pte. D. O'Neill

71483 Pte. A. Kearns
808181 Pte. T. Connolly
206011 Pte. P. Gildea
804740 Pte. J. Reynolds
92541 Pte. J. Hewitt

808440 Pte. J. Brady
802856 Pte. C. McManus
809853 Pte.G. Battles
98083 Pte. J. Mc.Evilly

4th F/Coy. SIGS.
802924 Cpl. E. Crocock

803746 Cpl. T. Doyle

803386 Cpl. T. Fleming

133

4thG/Coy. ACC.
92239 Sgt.J. Harris
804139 Pte. A. Rowe
807715 Pte. J. Geoghegan

803895 Pte. A. Tuohy
808074 Pte. G. Murtagh

808049 Pte. K. Lynch
809433 Pte. E. Spencer

4th F/Coy. S&T
803923 Pte. J. Mc.Court
810006 Pte. P. Donnelly
808976 Pte. T. Larkin
85949 Pte. W. Archbold

808283 Pte. M. Young
809012 Pte. C. Greevy
93700 Pte. W. Nally
06875 Pte. W. Deegan

808945 Pte. F. Newman
809804 Pte.J. Dunne
809388 Pte. D. Heagerty
803002 Pte. M. Hough

DOD Coy. Att. West Comd.
803366 Cpl. M. Kelly

809838 Pte. G. Morris

IV FA Regt.
86260 Pte. J. Harney
804539 Pte. P. Kelly
808012 Pte. J. Peppard
808470 Pte. M. Cahill
804870 Pte. J. Nugent

808472 Pte. M. Carroll
806874 Pte. J. Harvey
809871 Pte. M. Quinn
807247 Pte. T. Creevy

99848 Pte. M.Yates
807716 Pte. J. Nooney
91647 Pte. T. Scally
99886 Pte. E. Mc.Kenna

5th F/Coy. Sigs.
806951 Pte. D. Geraghty

CT. Depot West Comd.
89526 Sgt. J. Westman
808119 Pte. J. Doherty

802545 Sgt. J. Duke
90128 Pte. P. Shaughneassy

84096 Cpl. J. Kelly

4th Bde. Hqrs.
86531 Cpl. W. Dolan

807792 Pte. C. Fitzsimons

807971 Pte.T. Hanafin

4th G/Coy. MPC
803775 Cpl. T. Smith

805162 Cpl.M. O'Reilly

5th Motor Sqn.
803595 Cpl. B. Kiernan

805053 Cpl. N. Lambert

5th F/Coy. COE.
805400 Cpl. T. Bartley

802958 Cpl. P. Flaherty

5th FA Regt.
801217 Cpl. T. Gavin

807392 Cpl. H. Spenser

Western Comd. Hqrs.
807964 Pte. J. Broderick

806005 Pte. A. Molloy

3rd Inf. Bn.
431861 CQMS M. Kennedy
806088 Cpl. M. Kilty
808501 Pte. C. O'Rourke
806674 Pte. M. Mc.Loughlin
805666 Pte. P. Lawlor
808506 Pte. M. Daly
807017 Pte. J. Mehan
801104 Pte. M. Radford
808379 Pte. M. Gannon
96581 Pte. P. Furlong

87589 Sgt. T. Byrne
806850 Cpl. A. Colclough
807058 Pte. M. Whelan
801624 Pte. P. O'Neill
93856 Pte. M. Wynne
808377 Pte. D. Cooney
98364 Pte. A. France
803589 Pte. J. Doyle
807564 Pte. T. Sisk
07615 Pte. J. Grace

807071 Cpl. R. Mahon
806673 Cpl. T. Sheehan
807583 Pte. J. Larkin
808392 Pte. J. Delahunty
800019 Pte. A. Sheridan
803168 Pte. E. Kersting
806594 Pte. J. Caul
803541 Pte. M. Dingley
801123 Pte C. Sherry
807589 Pte. C. Doyle

Depot Signal Corps
96415 Sgt. N. Brick
93691 Cpl. L. Bevan
806252 Cpl. P. Gannon
806514 Pte. J. Hennessy

75963 Sgt. M. Quinn
91467 Cpl. D. Shine
807531 Cpl. M. O'Sullivan
808089 Pte. W. Redmond

802409 Sgt. A. Fogarty
804513 Cpl. P. Guckian
808094 Pte. J. Nolan

Camp Hqrs. CTC
79188 Sgt. P. Hayes
99913 Pte. S. White

801148 Sgt. J. Lawless

96103 Pte. P. Hayes

GT Depot, CTC
96939 Sgt. P. O'Neill
807114 Cpl. P. Cluskey
806241 Pte. J. Mallon

89829 Cpl. K. O'Rourke
809554 Pte. A. Breen
801105 Pte. M. Costello

803554 Cpl. R. Hamilton
809216 Pte. D. Noonan

1st H/Coy. AMC
88313 Cpl. P. Carroll
801189 Pte. T. Lacey

99926 Cpl. P. Durney
807668 Pte. P. McNair

807673 Pte. J. Mc.Nally

Depot S&T Corps
71074 Sgt. J. Madigan
88642 Pte. J. Flynn
89481 Pte. E. McGarahan

91756 Sgt. J. Rowe
800336 Pte. E. McGahey

806157 Cpl. F. Fogarty
98901 Pte. G. Fogarty

Depot Cav. Corps
96124 Sgt. J. Sexton
804743 Pte. J. Lucey

800347 Cpl. T. O'Connor
98485 Pte. M. Creevy

89893 Cpl. J. Mulcahy
98143 Pte. D. O'Halloran

Depot COE
422287 BQMS P. Harrington
804727 Cpl. S. Murphy
804696 Pte. F. Boland
804712 Pte. T. Fagan

804701 Cpl. P. Clancy
807662 Pte. N. Kelly
804718 Pte. A. Johnston
804299 Pte. P. Lynch

98361 Cpl. T. Carroll
809552 Pte. J. Coffey
804742 Pte. P. Sheerin

20th Inf. Bn.
807187 Cpl. P. Mc.Mahon

Depot AMC.
75881 Sgt. J. Gallagher
806225 Pte. J. McAdams
806699 Pte. T. Murphy

98984 Cpl. F. Fagan
806504 Pte. T. Murphy
809821 Pte. J. O'Donnell

801172 Cpl. J. Durney
807664 Pte. J. Hanlon

1st Tank Sqn.
86525 CQMS D. Nolan
80367 Cpl. J. O'Connor

76288 C/S M. Galvin
807151 Pte. K. Browne

87689 Sgt. P. Dignam
807221 Pte. E. Hackett

1st Armd. Sqn.
807101 Pte.M. Brown

808594 Pte. E. Gaffney

805380 Pte. A. Dunne

Iosta Cor Pa.
97558 Sgt. D. Bennett
98479 Cpl. C. Heavey

433933 Sgt. T. Dowse
81399 Cpl. J. Fleming

96833 Cpl. J. Chapman

1st AA Regt.
99729 Cpl. P. Doyle

99697 Cpl. J. O'Leary

1st G/Coy. AOC.
205132 C/S K. McCourt
92209 Cpl. P. Franey

98488 Sgt. M. Phelan
806552 Pte. J. Martin

95103 Sgt. P. Sludds

4th Motor Sqn.
804637 Cpl. T. Keogh
807168 Pte. J. Long

805715 Pte L. Ellard

807107 Pte. M. Noonan

AA Trg. Regt.
809070 Pte. J. Walsh

Air Corps
803067 A/M A. Raeside

2nd Inf. Bn.

92194 CQMS P. Bannon	87182 Sgt. P. Norris	95508 Sgt.J. Maguire
809457 Cpl. J. Roddy	803570 Cpl. M. Roche	808194 Cpl. J. Carroll
805894 Cpl. J. Walsh	808271 Cpl. R. Talbot	807077 Cpl. A. Duggan
806698 Cpl. J. Walsh	807676 Pte. E. Heffernan	93140 Pte. P. O'Brien
804907 Pte. C. Robinson	806363 Pte. J. Whelan	809775 Pte. J. Beresford
809694 Pte. S. Finnegan	807762 Pte. S. Glynn	809710 Pte. F. Howard
801776 Pte. J. Kelly	808730 Pte. M. Mason	803569 Pte. J. McMarlow
810442 Pte. M. Webster	808624 Pte. P. Browne	808647 Pte. J. Brennan
804393 Pte. B. Corbally	808968 Pte. S. Delaney	808998 Pte. W. McMahon
806984 Pte. H. Wright	807720 Pte. P. Corbally	804693 Pte. P. Murray
808274 Pte. J. Valentine	807682 Pte. P. Lackin	808807 Pte. F. Macklin
809364 Pte. D. McDonagh	807830 Pte. D. Russell	801078 Pte. P. Finlay
806375 Pte. J. Kelly	809372 Pte. W. O'Connor	807692 Pte. W. Smith
809792 Pte. M. Bishop	807900 Pte. F. Fox	807729 Pte. J. Hodgins
809033 Pte. J Hendrick	809430 Pte. J. Mahon	809711 Pte. N. McGrane
807680 Pte. R. O'Rourke	809001 Pte. M. Carey	803533 Pte. P. Barnes
806940 Pte. J. Barry	809367 Pte. O. Dixon	806936 Pte. G. Doyle
93995 Pte. W. O'Reilly	810422 Pte. J. Lawlor	804682 Pte. J. McGrath
807728 Pte. A. Martin	807209 Pte. S. Mc.Hugh	806965 Pte. L. O'Brien
800688 Pte. E. Richardson		

5 Inf. Bn.

405923 C/S J. Ryan	207944 Sgt. B. Fitzgerald	94912 Sgt. M. Hickey
803672 Cpl. N. Broe	807885 Cpl. J. Mc.Nair	809285 Cpl. G. Tyndall
807948 Cpl. J. Poland	806518 Cpl. A. Brennan	808841 Cpl. G. Bradley
807265 Cpl. E. Hamilton	808864 Cpl. H. O'Dea	809974 Pte. J. Buckley
810161 Pte. M. Dunphy	807286 Pte. L. Ellis	809619 Pte. J. Hardy
806466 Pte. P. Loftus	809965 Ptye. J. Murphy	808830 Pte. P. Newsome
807765 Pte. P. O'Brien	809150 Pte. R. White	807210 Pte. P. Byrne
807897 Pte. M. Davitt	804219 Pte. D. Hickey	809291 Pte. E. Mullen
809507 Pte. A. McNally	802740 Pte. E. Brady	807941 Pte. P. Doherty
803660 Pte. C. Johnston	803658 Pte. W. O'Brien	805714 Pte. M. Burke
807333 Pte. P. Guerin	97906 Pte. P. Davitt	808822 Pte. J. Browne
808466 Pte. T. Coyle	809246 Pte. R. Davis	809936 Pte. M. Fanning
807304 Pte. M. Kehoe	807267 Pte. J. Moran	809926 Pte. D. McConomy
807769 Pte. W. O'Reilly	808040 Pte. M. Whelan	807766 Pte. P. Mooney
88668 Pte. E. Connolly	809625 Pte. S. Gregory	809939 Pte. C. Murphy
809254 Pte. C. Mc.Donald	808683 Pte. E. McKenna	808041 Pte. M. Connole
802573 Pte. J. Doyle	802570 Pte. M. Lesley	807886 Pte. J. O'Sullivan
807909 Pte. J. Clifford	806209 Pte. P. Higgins	

7th Inf. Bn.
806525 Cpl. S. Reilly

8th Inf. Bn.
97951 Cpl. C. Jenkins

9th Inf. Bn.
91181 Cpl. J. Foley

21th Inf. Bn.
94834 Sgt. K. Power   806913 Cpl. J. Quinn

2nd F/Coy. Sigs.
404956 Sgt. P. Magorrian	803274 Cpl. W. Hughes	800945 Cpl. W. Beecher
806073 Cpl. E. 'Donoghue	809032 Pte. J. Duffy	808965 Pte. P. McCann
806310 Pte. J. Ryan	806540 Pte. A. Woodcock	807397 Pte. M. Duffy
807829 Pte. J. McGrath	09456 Pte. J. Ryan	

2nd Motor Sqn.
98598 Cpl. J. Garland	808001 Cpl. J. Aylward	808493 Cpl. J. Ward
807000 Pte S. Dodd	808877 Pte. C. Kavanagh	806182 Pte. J. McQuillan
807040 Pte. P. Freeman	807241 Pte. M. Kenny	808626 Pte. J. Birchall
808572 Pte. W. Flood	810561 Pte. T. Francis	805678 Pte. L. Murphy
808521 Pte. P. Nolan	802518 Pte. G. Hayes	808809 Pte. J. McCreanor
804356 Pte. A. Nugent		

2nd H/Coy. Amc.
211266 Pte. M. Hanna	808101 Pte. B. Byrne	804154 Pte. D. McKenzie
809189 Pte. P. Bergin	204540 Pte. W. Galligan	86106 Pte. T. Wolffe

2nd G/Coy. Mpc.
805797 Cpl. J. Waters	97615 Cpl. J. Doolan	93017 Cpl. J. White

2nd F/Coy. COE
71527 Sgt. J. Hanley	86759 Cpl. T. Doyle	802632 Cpl. W. Byrne
808549 Pte. O'Farrell		

2nd G/Coy. S&T
90094 Pte. C. Egan

2nd G/Coy. AOC
91722 Cpl. M. Cleary	807313 Pte. T. Lynch	806971 Pte. J. Donnelly

11th FA Regt.
804635 Cpl. P. Gallagher	806233 Pte. W. Deedy	804103 Pte. J. McKenna
804085 Pte. R. Roche	808328 Pte. O. Dennis	808311 Pte. J. McCooey
808314 Pte. P. Rock		

CT Depot E/Comd.
87729 Sgt. P. Keane	810689 Cpl. J. Flynn	801568 Cpl. T. Kelly
805588 Cpl. A. Carmody	78854 Pte. P. Madigan	809411 Pte. V. Lynch

DOD Coy. McKee Bks.
807809 Pte. J. Brennan	805416 Pte. D. Mooney	806647 Pte. W. Fitzpatrick
808422 Pte. J. Morrison		

2nd BDE Hqrs.
807981 Pte. G. Broggy	807864 Pte. R. Harmon

East Comd. Hqrs.
806444 Pte. M. Lester	805643 Pte. W. Sheridan

Clancy Bks. Coy.
98555 Cpl. J. Reddin

2nd F/Coy. S&T
95225 Cpl. J. Walsh

Depot ACC
90237 Cpl. M. Kavanagh

Personnel who served with the
33rd Battalion

(Rank at time of serving)

Bn HQ OC & Staff

Rev. Fr. John Crowley

0.5394 Comdt. K. O'Brien

0.7789 Lt. W.F. Raftery

Rev. Fr. Joseph Shinnors

0.6874 Comdt. E. J. Quigley

0.7208 Capt. I.J. Gibbons

0.4914 Lt/Col. R.W. Bunworth

0.5789 Capt. M.J. O'Donnell

'A' Platoon

0.4742 Comdt. J. McCarthy

0.5743 Capt. B.J. Gogarty

0.6536 Comdt. T.M. McMahon

05871 Capt. B.J. Basil

'Q' Section

0.5156 Comdt. P. Keogh

0.6689 Capt. M.J. Fitzgerald

0.7597 Capt. R. Sloane

Intelligence Section

0.4957 Comdt. P.D. Hogan

0.7331 Capt. R.A. Hinchy

Signal Section

0.7454 Capt. J. Gibbons

0.7720 Lt. K.M. Daly

Transport Section

0.7284 Capt. W. O'Flynn

0.7630 Lt. D.J. Byrne

Medical Section

0.5065 Comdt. J. Burke

0.7559 Comdt. J. Whelan

0.6740 Comdt. A. Beckett

0.5916 Comdt. B. Boyle

0.5028 Comdt. P. Heaney

'A' Company Group
Company Headquarters

0.6383 Comdt. L. Hogan

0.7168 Capt. J. Lavery

0.7353 Capt. D. Crowley

0.7412 Capt. J. Kelly

Rifle Platoon

0.7500 Lt. K. M. Gleeson

0.7511 Lt. J. Finucane

0.7617 Lt. C. P. O'Rourke

'B' Company Group
Company Headquarters

0.4938 Comdt. P. Barry

0.7373 Capt. P. J. Croke

0.6393 Capt. H. Gouldsborough

0.7423 Capt. J. Ryan

Rifle Platoon

0.7485 Lt. P. Condron

0.7493 Lt. J. Enright

0.7727 Lt. V. Blythe

'C' Company Group
Company Headquarters

0.4954 Comdt. T. Hanlon

0.7377 Capt. L. McMahon

0.6478 Capt. M. Crowley

0.7107 Capt. J. Flynn

Rifle Platoon

0.7490 Lt. J. Clarke

0.7494 Lt. A. McCarthy

0.7768 Lt. M. Bohan

Headquarters Company
'A' Platoon

58536 BSM D. Douglas	78964 CQMS J. Duggan	404311 C/S E. Keane
88672 Sgt. P. ushnan	90314 Sgt. J. Harrington	435871 Sgt. J. Barron
433820 Sgt. E. Whelan	76466 Sgt. J. Burke	89312 Sgt. G. O'Connor
74057 Sgt. M. Nolan	90255 Sgt. P. Farrell	92951 Cpl. T. Martin
94245 Cpl. J. Scully	800846 Cpl. J. Foran	809418 Cpl. D. Mannix
810040 Cpl. P. Curran	205650 Cpl. W. Peoples	802550 Cpl. Cullagh
217190 Cpl. L. Moran	804230 Cpl. D. Chaney	806154 Cpl. P. Kelly
89226 Cpl. E. O'Meara	802484 Pte. D. Sheehan	806871 Pte. M. Weston
806465 Pte. W. Church	800425 Pte. J. Stevenson	402157 Pte. W. Ambler
806578 Pte. T. Groarke	91695 Pte M. Bowe	808323 Pte. H. Marsh
808569 Pte.J. Forde	808598 Pte.J. Johnson	808352 Pte. K. Alcorn
805834 Pte. M. McCracken	806009 Pte. T. Gaffey	810082 Pte. C. McKeen
805365 Pte. V. Forde	808460 Pte. N. Foran	809511 Pte. T. Ryans
808247 Pte. J. Shields	106676 Pte. G. McSweeney	807139 Pte. Culhane
807173 Pte. Kenny	806219 Pte. Bourke	

'Q' Section

82957 BQMS C. McAllister	76589 C/S M. Maher	79939 CQMS T. Mullins
417528 Sgt. H. Bray	93854 Sgt. P. McCormack	435362 Sgt. W. McGrath
84284 Sgt. T. Murray	74863 Sgt. F. Mason	402644 Sgt. W. Dunne
804560 Cpl. J. McGivney	429646 Cpl. M. Lyons	801074 Cpl. C. Wren
209674 Cpl. J. Lynch	803932 Pte. T. McGuire	808347 Pte. P. Fortune
801691 Pte. E. Lynch	806441 Pte. T. Creagh	99913 Pte. J. White
99075 Pte. P. Houlihan	809767 Pte. P. Doyle	424180 Pte. J. Donnelly
93937 Pte T. Lynch	807969 Pte. J. McCaffrey	807279 Pte. L. Cortobelli
809783 Pte. D. Kearns	804715 Pte. P. Gilbride	809376 Pte. T. Crowley
96057 Pte. P. Wall		

Intelligence Section

96384 Sgt. M. Fenlon	97161 Sgt. J. Guthrie	91063 Cpl. F. Jones
98991 Cpl. M. 'Connor	807753 Cpl. T. Gavin	808156 Cpl. P. Curran
806640 Cpl. J. Reddy		

Signal Section

91116 Sgt. M. Sullivan	88148 Sgt. B. O'Keefe	805254 Cpl. T. Hurley
804509 Cpl. P. Cronin	804624 Pte. K. Dwyer	807928 Pte. N. Hoyne
808903 Pte. J. Quigley	806660 Pte. G. Windsor	809616 Pte. T. O'Regan
806513 Pte. P. Creighton		

Transport Section

801231 Sgt. M. Mulcahy	415292 Sgt. T. O'Dwyer	204987 Sgt. J. Hennessy
92233 Cpl. W. Kearns	96855 Cpl. A. Gannon	414453 Cpl. P. Heslin
805386 Cpl. M. Costello	412382 Pte. J. Talbot	803850 Pte. M. Fitzgerald
808375 Pte. M. McDermott	97241 Pte. P. Ryan	

Medical Section

79563 Sgt. P. Greensmyth	89816 Cpl. L. Hennessy	96723 Cpl. S. Flynn
800959 Pte. P. Gardiner	808438 Pte. J. Purcell	800760 Pte. P. Kingsley
806793 Pte. M. McCormack		

'A' Company

72811 C/S M. O'Brien	404399 CQMS A. Taylor	78922 Sgt. D. eating
88533 Sgt. J. Sexton	91470 Sgt. P. Keavey	804359 Sgt. H. Gaynor
94516 Sgt. K. Fogarty	803716 Sgt. P. O'Rourke	87631 Sgt. P. Duffy
809269 Cpl. H. Donovan	803674 Cpl. T. Crosbie	804202 Cpl. P. Grayley
90839 Cpl. J. Graham	808644 Cpl. M. Fitzhenry	800232 Cpl. J. Plunkett
88546 Cpl. E. Jameson	96506 Cpl. J. Smith	424848 Cpl. P. Roche
94169 Cpl. S. O'Byrne	95855 Cpl. M. Colton	808828 Cpl. J. O'Sullivan
803807 Cpl. J. Fitzgerald	808723 Cpl. P. O'Rourke	806079 Cpl. V. O'Grady

806304 Cpl. J. O'Sullivan
801988 Cpl. M. Monaghan
99803 Cpl. D. McGrath
807262 Cpl. H. Bulger
802413 Cpl. A. Kiernan
802448 Cpl. J. Hayden
801829 Cpl. T. Feeney
807813 Pte. V. Fitzpatrick
806112 Pte. A. Brown
805950 Pte. J. O'Carroll
806014 Pte. J. Murray
809146 Pte. J. Menton
804225 Pte. S. Henry
804536 Pte. M. Farrell
803884 Pte. M.J. Slemmon
93004 Pte. M. Bolger
808829 Pte. J. Bowes
802643 Pte. P. Browne
807205 Pte. F. Hyland
910166 Pte. J. Farrell
809271 Pte. T. Brady
809368 Pte. G. Geoghegan
809244 Pte. P. Rafferty
806643 Pte. P. Kennedy
808367 Pte. S. Menton
808520 Pte. C. Bolger
807186 Pte. C. Corbally
804344 Pte. P. Condra
90181 Pte. J. Kennedy
809696 Pte. J. Breen
808371 Pte. K. O'Neill
801730 Pte. M. Bartley
806479 Pte. M. Butler
809653 Pte. J. Cramp
808425 Pte. K. Donaghy
808491 Pte. J. Brady
806904 Pte. C. Cleary
808878 Pte. P. Kavanagh
805677 Pte. J. Kearns
105522 Pte. J. Purcell
807092 Pte. M. Smith
92065 Pte. J. Fitzgerald
806865 Pte. P. Miskella
809654 Pte. M. O'Reilly
809523 Pte. W. Hughes
809808 Pte. N. Byrne
807975 Pte. J. Griffin
808527 Pte. J. Traynor
808297 Pte. K. Murray
807130 Pte. D. Rogers
807810 Pte. D.Mc.Keown
806117 Pte. J. Byrne

93169 Cpl. M. Connell
807273 Cpl. P. Anderson
809839 Cpl. P. Kelly
804234 Cpl. L. Dougan
92785 Cpl. T. Scott
92176 Cpl. J. Murphy
800500 Cpl. J. Cummins
808351 Pte. F. Boyle
808802 Pte. L. Whelan
804736 Pte. J. O'Brien
91063 Pte. T. McAney
809642 Pte. W. Nolan
807945 Pte. J. Morrissey
808213 Pte. W. Mullin
809623 Pte. D. Carpenter
92963 Pte. S. Kelly
803789 Pte. J. Galvin
807167 Pte. N. Connolly
807060 Pte. P. Kirby
808799 Pte. J. Moore
809675 Pte. M. Cushnahan
808316 Pte. N. Williams
809371 Pte. W. Ryan
806753 Pte. N. Keogh
808427 Pte. J. Fallon
808601 Pte. N. Compton
807307 Pte. J. Walsh
803928 Pte. B. Dalton
807598 Pte. P. Feeney
808459 Pte. J. O'Brien
809469 Pte. H. Wood
06146 Pte E. Widdis
808346 Pte. N. Byrne
809954 Pte. J. Daly
806737 Pte. P. Donnelly
809257 Pte. D. Bradley
809485 Pte. F. Downes
808457 Pte. T. Kenny
808214 Pte. J. Fitzpatrick
809665 Pte. P. Denton
808292 Pte. F. Fenlon
805415 Pte. P. Fylan
808342 Pte. O. McAuley
808492 Pte. P. O'Toole
810085 Pte. D. Casey
804930 Pte. J. Farrell
807256 Pte. P. Lynch
809937 Pte. J. O'Sullivan
809519 Pte. J. Mullen
806379 Pte. D. Seagrave
807796 Pte. T. Murphy
808942 Pte. P. Hayes

807329 Cpl. J. Coombes
803670 Cpl. P. McDonald
809786 Cpl. J. Lynch
806558 Cpl. P. Mernagh
806234 Cpl. F. Nobel
77696 Cpl. W. Reidy
804358 Pte. J.J. O'Reilly
800992 Pte. J. Foley
808516 Pte. P. Murray
810242 Pte. G. Killeen
809846 Pte. P. Frawley
806145 Pte. G. Curran
211247 Pte. P. McGinn
807701 Pte. W. Bailey
211409 Pte. T. McLoughlin
807368 Pte. J. Cullen
807142 Pte. B. Boland
801374 Pte. J. Cush
809520 Pte. G. Buggy
809280 Pte. J. Kavanagh
808982 Pte. F. Dillon
809294 Pte. A. McMahon
93637 Pte. Bairnes
808487 Pte. P. Martin
808344 Pte. P. Flynn
94284 Pte. K. Hynes
93034 Pte. W. O'Brien
806867 Pte. F. Kenny
802900 Pte. M. McGuinn
808458 Pte. Stapleton
806805 Pte. A. Rafferty
806181 Pte. O. Fergus
808394 Pte. P. Molloy
806785 Pte. W.M. Davis
806741 Pte. J. Braddish
809621 Pte. E. Brennan
808548 Pte. T.F. Fennell
807062 Pte. D. McKenzie
95147 Pte. J. Kelly
808525 Pte. W. Duffy
809699 Pte. P. Fearon
809484 Pte. T. Fletcher
807162 Pte. J. Morris
808883 Pte. T. Kennedy
809970 Pte. J. McGinley
802770 Pte. J. Gallagher
807349 Pte. J. Smith
809620 Pte. W. Lawlor
809482 Pte. J. Moore
809148 Pte. D. Maxwell
809381 Pte. J.Burke
808444 Pte. G. Casey

'B' Company

80322 S/Com. F. Grant
99377 Sgt. P. Woods
91380 Sgt. M. Murphy
89619 Cpl. J. Moloney
805346 Cpl. P.O'Brien
801763 Cpl. A. Connolly

80122 CS/Com. P. Murphy
95600 Sgt. J. Dillon
209824 Sgt. W. Maher
804096 Cpl. M. McNamara
803483 Cpl. T. McCarthy
802969 Cpl. J. Dowling

204762 Sgt. J. Coy
86750 Sgt. M. Ryan
808159 Cpl. J.J. O'Connor
805256 Cpl. E. Fox
75051 Cpl. P. Byrne
90968 Cpl. P. Casey

808246 Cpl. T. Mulligan
803649 Cpl. W. McGee
96110 Cpl. W. Blake
807192 Cpl. C. Ryan
803540 Cpl. R. Dingley
802882 Cpl. C. McSweeney
80433 Cpl. W. O'Driscoll
94759 Cpl. R. Barry
96511 Cpl. K. Sludds
810645 Pte. J. Morrissey
809514 Pte. P. O'Sullivan
805687 Pte. J. Murphy
810238 Sgmn. G. Cleary
801981 Pte. E. Corcoran
801350 Pte. E. Kennedy
809027 Pte. W. Larkin
807015 Pte. J. Farrelly
806165 Pte. J. Roche
806213 Pte. P. Keogh
808439 Pte. P. Ryan
808200 Pte. C. Phillips
808463 Pte. J. Byrne
804804 Pte. P. Ryan
802301 Pte. J. Histon
808239 Tpr. J. Harris
809529 Pte. J. Cunningham
805486 Pte. G. McNamara
805448 Pte. A. Daly
808705 Pte. J. Delaney
808991 Pte. J. O'Malley
808672 Pte. J.Brennan
808560 Pte. P. Forde
805611 Pte. J. Roche
809201 Pte. M. Fitzgerald
807817 Pte. T. Clancy
806022 Pte. J. Murrihy
809702 Pte. F. O'Donnell
810053 Pte. J. Nugent
806149 Pte. Holden
805260 Pte. F. Cronin
803123 Pte. D. Horgan
809534 Pte. G. Long
808812 Pte. W. O'Mahony
808341 Pte. E.Murphy
809160 Pte. P. Sweeney
808659 Pte. P. Cahill
806340 Gnr. T. McElligott
807004 Pte. C. Maher
808462 Pte. J. Flynn
807003 Tpr. P. Doody
808612 Tpr. J. Kealy
808337 Tpr. P. Ryan
806688 Pte. J. Galvin
806962 Pte. J. Roche
806387 Pte. J. Smyth

'C' Company
91189 C/S M. O'Sullivan
87045 Sgt. L. Keane
93494 Sgt. P. Connelley

800227 Cpl. P. O'Sullivan
87429 Cpl. E. Fox
805189 Cpl. T. Kenneally
806918 Cpl. T. Considine
805446 Cpl. W. Whelan
805370 Cpl. A. Franklin
809356 Cpl. P. Kent
802295 Cpl. B. Griffin
804776 A/M P. McGoldrick
95024 Pte. E. Ryall
805121 Pte. T. McCarthy
415841 Pte. J. Guerin
808127 Pte. E. Lonergan
75786 Pte. W. Flood
800786 Pte. M. Hurley
808895 Pte. W. Flynn
806798 Pte. T. Wright
800600 Pte. J. Kelly
806322 Pte. J. McNamara
808176 Pte. J. McCoy
807959 Pte. M. Moynihan
803635 Pte. T. Leehey
805447 Pte. T. McGrath
804418 Pte. T. Nagle
808559 Pte. J. Mitchell
808892 Pte. M. O'Shea
809024 Pte. E. Ryan
806133 Pte. J. Eviston
808132 Pte. T. Campbell
808129 Pte. T. Corrigan
808889 Pte. S. Donnellan
809343 Pte. M. Fogarty
808476 Pte. J. Cribben
806662 Gnr. P. McNamara
803793 Pte. M. O'Sullivan
804874 Pte. P. O'Connor
806008 Pte. F. Corbett
809278 Pte. P. J. Cuddihy
806677 Pte. Maher
806142 Pte. J. Brassil
804568 Pte. P. Roche
801694 Pte. T. Broe
99221 Gnr. E. Stokes
808340 Pte. D. Cambridge
802765 Pte. F. O'Connor
808866 Pte. M. Laste
809183 Pte. C. McGrath
805510 Pte. M. Roche
98426 Tpr. A. Enright
810339 Tpr. O'Callaghan
808980 Tpr. D. Pierce
803355 Pte. M. Brennan
808936 Pte. B. Hoare
809116 Pte. P. Roberts
802736 Pte. G. Costelloe

75915 CSC P.A. Dillon
87555 Sgt. T.M. Conlon
79185 Sgt. T. Wilson

800128 Cpl. E. Barnes
803648 Cpl. W. McMahon
808284 Cpl. M. Byrnes
802255 Cpl. J. O'Sullivan
806390 Cpl. A. O'Neill
808124 Cpl. T. Leahy
802172 Cpl. T. Cunningham
99625 Cpl. T. Murray
808309 Pte. M. Bowler
98933 Pte. S. Gleeson
809239 Pte. J. Hogan
87262 Pte. R. Downey
809930 Sgmn. Hurley
93234 Pte. L. Kelliher
803931 Pte. J. Mulcahy
806629 Pte. M. Jordan
808602 Tpr. D. Keegan
809894 Pte. D. Walsh
806191 Pte. E. Burke
808144 Pte. C. Maher
808640 Pte. J. Ryan
96372 Pte. E. Power
806192 Pte. J. O'Brien
808269 Pte. B. Halvey
809465 Pte. M. Hartigan
805192 Pte. J. Kennedy
810556 Pte. M. O'Brien
810413 Pte. M. Cleary
808437 Pte. E. Noonan
808330 Pte. M. Hickey
808286 Pte. G. Ledger
808478 Pte. J. McMahon
808911 Pte. M. Power
800645 Pte. K. McNamara
807381 Gnr.E. McGrath
805609 Pte. M. Ward
804157 Pte. J. Boyce
800586 Pte. P. Fennessey
806944 Pte. R. Whelan
808955 Pte. T. Brett
97957 Pte. E. McMahon
808709 Pte. P. Mahony
809395 Tpr. T. O'Keeffe
807310 Pte. J. McGrath
809374 Pte. M. Cotter
802377 Gnr.A. Madden
808557 Gnr. J. O'Callaghan
809498 Gnr. P. O'Connell
805148 Tpr. J.J. O'Connor
809658 Tpr. J. O'Sullivan
808804 Tpr. A. Mulhern
806148 Pte. M. Walsh
809493 Pte. T. Hurley
809958 Pte. T. O'Regan

92195 Sgt. M. Hamill
200920 Sgt. M. Ambrose
99093 Sgt. J. Hamill

805210 Cpl. J. Price
809326 Cpl. J. Allen
86692 Cpl. J. O'Reilly
804646 Cpl. F. O'Sullivan
805225 Cpl. Whitley
802604 Cpl. J. Redmond
807063 Cpl. T. Durney
807528 Cpl. P. Ronan
805042 Cpl. R. Hall
436149 Cpl. J. King
805626 Cpl. J. Broderick
95878 Cpl. M. Timpson
804799 Cpl. P. Flanagan
436293 Pte. J. Salmon
810627 Pte. B. Smullen
802147 Pte. S. Costello
91330 Pte. J. Kearney
805252 Pte. N. Kavanagh
808228 Pte. S. Coogan
808216 Pte. J. O'Shea
803160 Pte. T. Bevan
805587 Pte. J. Kenny
806503 Pte. V. Lakes
807010 Pte. O. Walsh
808224 Pte. N. Kinsella
806960 Pte. J. McGuire
808030 Pte. T. Murphy
809444 Pte. K. Mahon
807603 Pte. B. Hickey
809540 Pte. S. Harris
808919 Pte. L.Walsh
808383 Pte. S. Carroll
807675 Pte. B. Hackett
806568 Pte. P. Rossiter
807588 Pte. J. Conroy
806993 Pte. D. Rafferty
808380 Pte. J. Hayden
807031 Pte. P. Landers
807069 Pte. P. Flood
809455 Pte. P. Keyes
809074 Pte. J. Doran
806659 Pte. F. Drohan
803387 Pte. S. Nolan
808411 Pte. P. Quirke
806621 Pte. O. Connerny
806670 Pte. E. Gorey
808499 Pte. P. Moran
807577 Pte. J. Dolan
808497 Pte. M. Nolan
803754 Pte. W. Canning
808232 Pte. E. Jordan
807660 Pte. Lawless
808032 Pte. T. Gainfort
807600 Pte. T. Gates
806170 Pte. P. Murphy
809436 Pte. M. Ryan
806043 Pte. T. Broe
808930 Pte. J. Ryan
808388 Pte. P. Goggin

806417 Cpl. J. O'Neill
804967 Cpl. B. Smith
91460 Cpl. M. McDonagh
86692 Cpl. J. O'Reilly
99814 Cpl. J. Kelly
806855 Cpl. L. Kelly
808393 Cpl. M. Lambert
808385 Cpl. M. Conway
806836 Cpl. J. Kennedy
804877 Cpl. J. Ging
806669 Cpl. P. Folan
808567 Cpl. T. Bolger
809727 Pte. N. McGlynn
108400 Pte. M. O'Sullivan
804697 Pte. J. Brennan
809344 Pte. T. McCarthy
806152 Pte. M. Anderson
807843 Pte. N. Jordan
806243 Pte. P. Hayde
808894 Pte. T. Cronin
809219 Pte. D. Fortune
808496 Pte. G. Coleman
808022 Pte. K. Colbert
807065 Pte. P. Mullalley
808229 Pte. P. O'Halloran
99423 Pte. J. Flynn
806083 Pte. M. Caffrey
806169 Pte. F. Morrissey
807656 Pte. S. Dempsey
809443 Pte. J. Leigh
806596 Pte. N. McGuinness
98731 Pte. P. Casey
806884 Pte. W. Bolger
807076 Pte. K. Keedy
90597 Pte. S. Caffrey
806424 Pte. W. Delaney
808508 Pte. C. Ennis
99070 Pte. J. Rafter
800768 Pte. E. Goff
807534 Pte. J. Williams
808403 Pte. P. Dreeling
805793 Pte. J. Byrne
808515 Pte. P. Rooney
808225 Pte. P. King
808762 Pte. D. Dempsey
803578 Pte. R. Hall
808415 Pte. P. Whelan
806854 Pte. J. Connolly
807067 Pte. A. Hickey
808395 Pte. C. Curran
807075 Pte. P. Cahill
805784 Pte. M. Walsh
807137 Pte. C. Gleeson
801913 Pte. P. Cullen
809827 Pte. D. Conway
808396 Pte. M. Clancy
808785 Pte. J. Caulfield
807079 Pte. W. Tyrell
808017 Pte. D. McLaurence

98484 Cpl. S. Graham
806024 Cpl. J. Hand
804625 Cpl. T. O'Connor
808348 Cpl. T. O'Hara
808502 Cpl. J. Lockeman
806368 Cpl. M. Lysaght
810333 Cpl. M. Byrne
803552 Cpl. G. Cullen
805250 Cpl. T. Sweeney
807390 Cpl. P. Kavanagh
808916 Cpl. P. Sparrow
93256 Pte. J. Phoenix
88097 Pte. P. Hannigan
78361 Pte. C. Doolan
95462 Pte. T. Doheney
803352 Pte J. Maguire
807665 Pte. N. Burke
801355 Pte. M. Hurley
430446 Pte. J. Moran
810169 Pte. P. Cosgrove
803023 Pte. F. Griffin
808397 Pte. M. Donohue
809022 Pte. P. O'Brien
803743 Pte. P. Byrne
77597 Pte. J. O'Regan
806275 Pte. T. Talbot
88044 Pte. M. Cuddy
808016 Pte. T. Arrigan
807013 Pte. S. Glasheen
807380 Pte. J. Lafferty
807580 Pte. T. Kealy
809719 Pte. O'Neill
99384 Pte. R. McSweeney
808410 Pte. F. Harris
809725 Pte. P. Foley
808227 Pte. B. Deegan
98448 Pte. J. Canavan
807064 Pte. D. Reid
809221 Pte. D. Finn
809230 Pte. A. Costello
808504 Pte. E. Donohue
808412 Pte. J. Nolan
807056 Pte. J. Phillips
801136 Pte. W. Bohan
806557 Pte. T. Fortune
801821 Pte. J. Canning
81438 Pte. T. Cullinane
806995 Pte. D. O'Rourke
801830 Pte. J. Kelly
808220 Pte. T. Daly
807920 Pte. M. Kenny
807837 Pte. C. O'Neill
807032 Pte. P. Green
804415 Pte. T. McGuire
809549 Pte. T. Goffe
807574 Pte. J. Kenny
808923 Pte. D. Rochford
807143 Pte. T. Kelly